PROBLEMS
AND SIMULATIONS
IN EVIDENCE
Fourth Edition

PROBLEMS AND SIMULATIONS IN EVIDENCE

Fourth Edition

Thomas F. Guernsey
President and Dean
Albany Law School

ISBN: 9781422478974

Library of Congress Cataloging-in-Publication Data
Guernsey, Thomas F.
Problems and simulations in evidence / Thomas F. Guernsey. -- 4th ed.
p. cm.
Includes index.
ISBN 978-1-4224-7897-4 (softbound)
1. Evidence (Law)--United States--Problems, exercises, etc. I. Title.
KF8935.Z9G84 2010
347.73'6--dc22   2010017253

NOTE TO USERS

To ensure that you are using the latest materials available in this area, please be sure to periodically check the LexisNexis Law School web site for downloadable updates and supplements at www.lexisnexis.com/lawschool.

Editorial Offices

121 Chanlon Rd., New Providence, NJ 07974 (908) 464-6800
201 Mission St., San Francisco, CA 94105-1831 (415) 908-3200
www.lexisnexis.com

MATTHEW◆BENDER

DEDICATION

For Kathe, Alison and Adam.

TABLE OF CONTENTS

TABLE OF CONTENTS

INTRODUCTION

The publications **Best Practices for Legal Education: A Vision and a Road Map** (CLEA 2007) and the Carnegie Foundation for the Advancement of Teaching's **Educating Lawyers: Preparation for the Profession** (Jossey-Bass 2007) have now joined the ranks of the McCrate Report and Crampton Report in calling for fundamental change in the way legal education is delivered. Evidence teachers have consistently been in the forefront in advancing the goals of these reports by teaching skills and values, integrating practice with the theoretical, and providing multiple formative as well as summative assessments. While the First Edition of this book was written well before either Carnegie or Best Practices, many of the themes are seen throughout the book.

To integrate skills and values, each chapter includes realistic examples of how the evidentiary rule is used in practice. For example, many problems are put in the context of witness examinations (often word for word from transcripts). While evidence obviously is primarily concerned with the admissibility in court, it is misleading to assume that the courtroom is the only place where evidence issues are addressed, and that only trial attorneys need to be concerned with such issues. Many of the problems and simulations, therefore, involve interviewing, counseling, negotiation, fact investigation, office policies and the like.

Using both problems and simulations, these materials are designed to teach you to approach evidence in a systematic manner; to analyze both legal doctrine and the factual setting in which that doctrine works. Perhaps the most unique aspect of these materials is the use of simulations. Even in a course like evidence in which faculty have used simulation for many years, most of the simulations used have been set in the courtroom. These traditional simulations usually involve direct and cross-examinations. In addition, most traditional simulations are done in the classroom.

While many of the simulations contained in this book are done in the classroom and involve direct and cross-examination, many others involve non-courtroom situations and are designed to be performed outside the classroom. Many of the simulations performed outside the classroom are followed by questionnaires. When these questionnaires are answered after the exercise, they should provide immediate feedback on your understanding of the evidentiary principles involved. Your answers also allow your instructor to judge if the class is having difficulty with the material.

Many of the problems and simulations involve one of the basic fact patterns found in Appendices A–C. Problems beginning *State v. Duffy* refer to Appendix A; *Donato v. Donato* refers to Appendix B; and *Paula v. David and PDG* refers to Appendix C. Where dates involve multiple years, the convention of "Yr —" is used. For example, Yr-0 is the present year and Yr-1 is last year.

This edition of Problems and Simulations also contains two Performance Tests. The majority of bar applicants in the United States now take at least one performance test on the bar examination. It seems appropriate where possible, therefore, to expose to students the type of examination that they most likely will take. I originally wrote these Performance Tests for the California bar examination as a member of its

INTRODUCTION

Performance Test Editing Team. The team then edited and pretested the items prior to their administration. I want to express my appreciation to the Committee of Bar Examiners of the State of California for allowing me to reproduce these items.

Finally, I would like to thank several people for help in developing these materials. First, my wife, Kathe Klare, provided me with the special expertise of a nurse-lawyer familiar with both malpractice and laws affecting people with disabilities. Her influence will be seen throughout. Barbara Britzke and I many years ago created the broad outline of the Donato family. The Donato family difficulties, in several different contexts, have engaged students at several law schools for the past ten years. Finally, I would like to renew my thanks to Tony Bocchino and Joe Harbaugh. Tony taught me evidence and how to be a trial lawyer. Joe taught me how to be a teacher.

Chapter 1

RELEVANCY

1.1 For each of the following items of proposed evidence, identify the possible factual hypotheses toward which it could be offered and determine whether the evidence should be admissible under Federal Rule of Evidence 401 or under the common law.

.1 In a prosecution for homicide, the prosecutor seeks to introduce evidence that on two occasions the defendant stated he intended to kill the victim.

.2 In an action to quite title, Al claims title by adverse possession. Al seeks to introduce the testimony of two teenagers who will testify that they were told by Al, "Get off this property, it's mine."

.3 Defendant is charged with illegal importation and distribution of narcotics. The government seeks to introduce evidence that defendant was seen in possession of a gun during the time of the alleged criminal activities.

.4 *State v. Duffy.* At Arlo's trial, there is testimony that a chrome plated .38 caliber gun was used in the bank robbery. The prosecutor now seeks to introduce testimony of a neighbor of Arlo's. Although she does not know what type of gun it was, the neighbor will testify that she saw the defendant carrying a bright, shiny gun into his apartment two weeks before the robbery. Assume she saw the gun two years before the robbery. Would that affect your answer? Assume Arlo will testify that, at the time the neighbor saw him, he had just purchased a set of toy guns for his nephew. Would that change your answer?

.5 In a product liability action alleging a defective football helmet, plaintiff claims permanent brain damage resulting in severe emotional problems. These problems, he alleges, include the fact that he is no longer socially active, and that when he does participate in an activity he becomes inordinately tired. The defendant seeks to introduce evidence of plaintiff's post injury sexual and gambling activities.

.6 Defendant, a police officer, is sued for violating plaintiff's civil rights during an arrest. Defendant seeks to introduce evidence that plaintiff was using cocaine at the time of the arrest.

.7 Assume that in the preceding problem defendant seeks to introduce a picture of a weapon that is allegedly owned by plaintiff. Is it admissible? Would it affect your answer if there has not yet been testimony that plaintiff had a gun the night of the arrest?

.8 In a prosecution for knowingly receiving stolen property, the prosecutor seeks to introduce evidence that immediately before defendant made his purchase five other people refused to purchase the property in question. Each of the five people will testify that they believed the property was stolen. Would it make a difference if the five other people were co-workers with the defendant?

.9 In a workman's compensation case, claimant slipped and fell in a puddle of water. Claimant seeks to introduce testimony that her employer was seen mopping up a puddle in the same location just two hours before she was injured.

.10 Defendant is charged with knowingly and willfully making false statements on a passport application. Defendant wishes to introduce evidence that he made the false statements in an attempt to speed up the passport application process so that he could visit his dying mother overseas.

.11 In a defamation action, defendant is alleged to have called the plaintiff, a minister, a "crook." Defendant seeks to introduce evidence that the plaintiff's reputation in the community is that he had frequent affairs with members of his congregation. If the court admits the evidence, what should the plaintiff seek to have the jury instructed?

.12 *Paula v. David and PDG.* Paula seeks to introduce evidence that PDG has liability insurance.

.13 Plaintiff sues a drug manufacturer in an action for personal injury. Under appropriate state law, plaintiff seeks compensation for physical injury, pain, suffering, and punitive damages. Plaintiff seeks to introduce copies of the defendant's financial records, including income tax returns for the preceding five years.

.14 *Paula v. David and PDG.* Walter testified that David had the green light. On cross-examination, Brewster asks, "Isn't it true that immediately after the accident you told police officer Kelly that my client, Paula, had the green light?"

.15 During the same cross-examination as in the previous problem, Brewster also asks, "Isn't it true that two years ago you had a fight with my client at the Triangle Tavern?"

.16 Following the cross-examination that took place in the two previous problems, Marla asks on redirect examination, "Would you tell the jury why you had the fight with the plaintiff?" If allowed, the answer will indicate a long-standing grudge between the witness and the plaintiff resulting from the plaintiff having fired Walter from a job.

.17 *Paula v. David and PDG.* Paula calls Wanda to the stand and asks, "How long have you lived here in town?"

.18 *State v. Duffy.* The prosecutor seeks to offer evidence that one hour after the robbery Arlo fled when he was approached on the street by police officers. When apprehended, Arlo told the police officer that his name was Ryan Clooney. Assume the flight occurred five months after the robbery. Would that change your answer?

.19 In the previous problem, would it make any difference if it had been reported in the newspapers that Arlo was being sought in connection with a liquor store robbery? Would it make a difference if the newspaper indicated Arlo was sought in connection with a bank robbery?

.20 The state government began condemnation proceedings against a landowner's property, and introduced testimony by an expert appraiser that the landowner's property is worth $100,000. The landowner seeks to introduce testimony from a local real estate agent that in the past three years five houses have been sold in same neighborhood, each for a price in excess of $110,000.

1.2 For each of the following pieces of evidence, identify the possible factual hypotheses toward which it could be offered and whether the evidence should be admissible under Federal Rules of Evidence 401 and 403, or the common law.

.1 Plaintiff sued defendant for running him over with his car as he attempted to cross an intersection. Plaintiff seeks to introduce a color photograph of him that shows him on the street with blood flowing from his head.

.2 Plaintiff, a nationally known religious/political figure, sues the owner of a men's magazine for defamation and invasion of privacy. The allegedly defamatory comments were made in the magazine in the context of an advertising parody. Plaintiff seeks to introduce the entire magazine, containing numerous "hard core" pictures of people in various stages of undress and sexual activity.

.3 In defendant's trial for illegal possession of marijuana, the prosecutor seeks to introduce expert testimony concerning the effects of the drug.

.4 A border patrol officer is charged with obtaining sexual favors from illegal aliens in return for allowing them to enter the country. The defendant seeks to introduce evidence that the illegal aliens were formerly employed as prostitutes.

.5 Plaintiff's son died, allegedly from inhaling a household product made by the defendant. Defendant seeks to introduce evidence of the son's marijuana use.

.6 Plaintiff sued the manufacturer of an automobile for personal injuries, alleging a design defect. Plaintiff seeks to introduce the longitudinal cross section of a new car of the same model in an attempt to show the jury the manufacturing defect.

.7 Defendant is charged with the murder of his wife and two children. Defendant claims that drug crazed people broke into his house the night of the murders, and that, after he was unsuccessful in fighting them off, they killed his family. The prosecutor requests the judge allow the jury to view the defendant's home where the murders occurred.

.8 *Paula v. David and PDG.* Paula's attorney asks the judge to allow the jury to go to the intersection and view the accident scene.

.9 In a product liability action, plaintiff claims his leg was severed when defendant's machine malfunctioned. Plaintiff seeks to exhibit his leg to the jury.

.10 In an action against defendant for child abuse, the prosecutor seeks to introduce color photographs of the child showing bruises and cigarette burns.

.11 Defendant is charged with receiving illegal "kickbacks" from vendors. Defendant wishes to call 78 vendors who will each testify that defendant did not solicit kickbacks from them, and that they did not pay any kickbacks to the defendant.

.12 Defendant was founder and president of a nonprofit daycare center that received reimbursement from the federal government for serving meals to disadvantaged children. The government claims the defendant received $13.5 million more than she was entitled to over a five-year period. Defendant is charged with mail fraud and embezzling. The government seeks to introduce evidence of defendant's purchase of expensive jewelry, clothing, and trips to Las Vegas for gambling, where she arranged large lines of credit prior to arrival. A government agent estimates her expenditures during the indictment period at $3,896,939.

.13 Defendant and other co-defendants were indicted on one count of conspiracy to possess with intent to distribute and to distribute methamphetamine. The indictment alleges that defendant, along with the other co-defendants, obtained significant quantities of methamphetamine from Christopher for resale and distribution. Christopher is the leader of a gang called "Villa Lobos." Defendant denies being a member of Villa Lobos. One of the co-defendants will testify that defendant told him that he got a tattoo bearing the name "Villa Lobos" to "cement his business relationship."

The prosecution seeks to introduce evidence that defendant has a tattoo bearing the name "Villa Lobos."

1.3 Plaintiff brings suit against two police officers for conspiring to and actually then violating her constitutional rights. Plaintiff was arrested at a rally where she and several hundred others were protesting the President of the United States. Defendants file a motion in limine seeking to exclude the following evidence. How should the court rule?

.1 Any evidence of allegedly wrongful conduct by police offers other than the defendants in this matter.

.2 Plaintiff's video evidence showing the arrest. The defendants argue that the evidence is substantially outweighed by its probative value.

1.4 The defendant is charged with conspiracy under the Racketeer Influenced and Corrupt Organizations Act (RICO) as well as a separate count of kidnapping-torture. The RICO count alleges racketeering acts including numerous conspiracies to murder, murders and a conspiracy to kidnap and kidnappings. Among the uncharged acts in this RICO conspiracy was the alleged murder of John Favara, and defendant's role as an accessory to that murder by disposing of Favara's body by dissolving it in acid. Three witnesses, if allowed, will testify that the defendant told them that he disposed of many bodies, including Favara's, for his boss by placing the bodies in barrels of acid and storing them on property next to his junkyard. At trial, the government seeks to present the following evidence. Is it admissible under Federal Rules of Evidence 401, 402 and 403?

.1 Testimony concerning the defendant's use of acid in the disposal of bodies.

.2 Testimony concerning the use of acid in the torture of the kidnapping for which he was specifically charged.

.3 A videotape of the kidnapping victim showing damage done to his feet by the acid.

1.5 Defendants are on trial for conspiracy to damage, and destroy by fire, a building used in interstate commerce and of actually damaging and destroying the building. The prosecution seeks, over defendants' objection, to show that the building in question had four other fires over a three-year period.

.1 Under what circumstances, if any, should evidence of these four fires be admitted? What is the judge's role in making this determination of admissibility?

.2 If the trial court admits the evidence, what should defense counsel do to preserve her objection for appeal?

.3 Assume the court conducted a *voir dire* hearing on the issue. If the defendant testifies during this hearing denying any connection with the four previous fires, has the defendant waived his right to refuse to testify concerning whether he committed the crime for which he is now being tried?

.4 Should this *voir dire* examination take place in the presence of the jury?

1.6 Plaintiff, a black woman, was an hourly employee at defendant's manufacturing plant. She had 12 years seniority. Plaintiff was involved in a fight at work with two white co-workers. As a result of the fight, plaintiff was fired. Neither of the co-workers was discharged. Prior to the present action, plaintiff had received no reprimands or any form of discipline. After exhausting administrative remedies, plaintiff brought the present action, alleging that her discharge was discriminatory.

Over objection by the defendant, plaintiff introduced evidence of fights involving other employees of the defendant. She alleges that the evidence demonstrates a pattern of disparate treatment against racial minorities by the defendant. This evidence included:

- A fight between a black male and a white male that took place ten years earlier. There was conflicting evidence as to who started the fight. Company records show that after the two men exchanged heated words, the black man struck the white man, and the white man swung a wild blow at the other, but missed hitting him. The Company then discharged both men, but later reinstated the white man, reducing his penalty to a 30-day suspension.

- Two white employees were involved in a fight nine years ago. One was hospitalized. Both were suspended.

- Eight years ago a white employee struck co-worker who was also white, "after provocation," according to company records. The employee was suspended for one week.

- Seven years ago a Mexican American hit a white employee, in the face. The company discharged the Mexican-American employee, though both employees told the company that they were merely goofing around.

- Two black employees were engaged in a fight six years ago. One was given a four-day suspension.

- A white male had a fight with his supervisor two years ago and was subsequently given a one day disciplinary layoff.

The jury returned a verdict for plaintiff. In granting defendant's motion for a judgment notwithstanding the verdict, the trial court stated:

The evidence of past incidents was irrelevant. Of the thirteen employees discussed by the plaintiff in her case-in-chief, only two are truly similarly situated to the plaintiff — all three, including plaintiff, were unprovoked aggressors. None of the other eleven employees were involved in similar circumstances, mainly because none of the eleven but Robinson was adjudged by the defendant an aggressor. Based on these conclusions, I hold that plaintiff presented absolutely no evidence that met the test of relevance.

.1 Is plaintiff's evidence relevant?

.2 Is it appropriate to rule the evidence admissible during plaintiff's case-in-chief and then to reverse that decision in ruling on the motion for the judgment notwithstanding the verdict?

.3 Reread the trial court's rationale; does it suggest some confusion as to the appropriate role of the judge *vis-a-vis* the jury?

.4 Assume that on appeal the appellate court rules that some of the evidence is admissible, but should be excluded under Federal rule of Evidence 403. On appeal to the United States Supreme Court, how should the Court rule?

1.7 Plaintiffs brought suit alleging sexual harassment by an employee of the defendant, a fast food franchise operator. Plaintiffs allege that after receiving numerous complaints of inappropriate behavior toward female employees, defendant transferred the employee to another restaurant location. The plaintiffs allege that the employee engaged in inappropriate sexual behavior toward female employees, including inappropriate touching and making inappropriate comments. Plaintiffs also allege that they reported the employee's conduct to supervisors who did little in response until the defendant finally terminated the employee for an incident in which he allegedly touched one of the plaintiff's inappropriately. The parties filed a number of motions in limine before trial. How should the judge rule on each motion?

> **.1** The first motion seeks to exclude evidence of one of the plaintiff's felony convictions for possession of marijuana pipes and use of marijuana. Defendants argue that the evidence is relevant to the employee's failure to mitigate damages and is, therefore, relevant to any claim for back pay.

> **.2** A second motion seeks to exclude evidence of drug and alcohol use by one of the plaintiffs. The motion argues that such evidence is irrelevant and highly prejudicial. Defendants respond by arguing that evidence of drug and alcohol use is relevant to the claimants' ability to recollect events at issue in this case and to their claim for emotional distress damages.

> **.3** Defendant filed a motion to bar testimony and evidence that the employee who allegedly acted inappropriately frequented sex clubs.

1.8 Plaintiff was convicted of sexual abuse of a child and served a term of imprisonment. Upon his release he was committed for a two-year term as a Sexually Violent Predator (SVP). The commitment is based in part on a finding that plaintiff cannot control his behavior and as such presents a substantial risk of violence to others. Plaintiff brings this action seeking damages under 42 U.S.C. § 1983 arguing that the conditions of his confinement violated his constitutional rights because his confinement was more onerous than confinement suffered by other civil and pre-trial detainees. The Court entered summary judgment in favor of plaintiff, reserving for trial the issue of damages. Prior to trial on the damage issue, plaintiff files a motion in limine seeking to preclude the introduction of evidence of his status as a Sexually Violent Predator. How should the court rule?

1.9 FACT INVESTIGATION. *State v. Duffy.* You have just been assigned to prosecute Arlo Duffy. You must now begin your fact investigation of the case. You will need to tell the investigators what they should look for. Identify the key legal or factual propositions or hypotheses crucial to both prosecuting and defending the bank robbery charge. Itemize the specific evidence from witnesses as well as the demonstrative and physical evidence you expect the investigator to gather relating to each of these factual propositions. Be sure to indicate where and how the investigator should look for this evidence.

1.10   FACT INVESTIGATION. *Donato v. Donato.* You represent Gina. You must now begin your fact investigation of the case. You will need to instruct the investigators on what they should look for. Identify the key legal or factual propositions crucial to both the mother and father in the custody case. Itemize the specific evidence from witnesses as well as the demonstrative and physical evidence you expect the investigator to gather relating to these factual propositions. Be sure to indicate where and how he should look for this evidence.

1.11   CLOSING ARGUMENT. *State v. Duffy.* You represent Arlo. Based on the material contained in the *State v. Duffy* file, make your *closing* argument to the jury.

1.12   LEGISLATIVE DRAFTING. You work for a state legislator on a committee considering the adoption of rules of evidence modeled after the Federal Rules. The legislator has asked you to consider the appropriateness of redrafting Federal Rule 401's "any tendency" language with language setting a higher standard for determining probative value. Prepare to discuss this with the legislator, being sure to consider whether such a revision is appropriate, and, if the legislator determines it is, what the standard ought to be and how the rule should be rewritten.

Chapter 2

COMPETENCY, PERSONAL KNOWLEDGE, AND OATH OR AFFIRMATION

2.1 BASIC COMPETENCY CONCEPTS.

.1 Six-year-old Alice was allegedly raped by her father. The father is on trial. Should Alice be allowed to testify? What factors should go into the decision as to whether she may testify?

.2 *State v. Duffy.* Before his arrest, the police received a tip from Beatrice Duke that Arlo had told her he had committed the robbery. Beatrice takes the stand, and defense counsel objects to her testimony on the ground that she is incompetent to testify because she is addicted to heroin. Assuming she is addicted, how should the judge rule?

.3 *State v. Duffy.* Arlo takes the stand and denies all involvement in the robbery. During the cross-examination of Arlo, the judge interjects the following:

> Q: Excuse me, Mr. Duffy. Didn't you call me about a week before your arrest?
>
> A: Yes, your honor.
>
> Q: You came by my office too?
>
> A: Yes, sir.
>
> Q: You wanted help?
>
> A: I haven't ever been in trouble like this.
>
> Q: I told you to simply tell the truth, didn't I?
>
> A: Yes.
>
> Q: You said you couldn't because other people were involved?
>
> A: I think, as best I can remember, that I told you the same as I testified today.
>
> Q: But you told me a different story then didn't you?

Was this questioning proper? If not, what should defense counsel do?

.4 In a criminal prosecution, the defendant moved for a mistrial claiming the defendant was denied the presumption of innocence. To support the motion, defense counsel seeks to call as a witness a juror sitting in the case. The juror, if allowed, will testify that she saw the defendant in the parking lot of the courthouse during a lunch break. At the time, the defendant was wearing handcuffs. May the juror testify?

.5 Following a guilty verdict in a federal criminal prosecution, a member of the jury contacted defense counsel. The juror told counsel that she was sorry the defendant was convicted. The foreman of the jury, however, scared her to death with his demands that a decision be made and his unwillingness to accept any discussion that the defendant was not guilty. In an attempt to set aside the verdict, defense counsel seeks to call this former juror as a witness. Should the judge allow the testimony? Assume the juror told defense counsel that the foreman had brought in copies of the newspaper during deliberations and used press accounts to support his argument that the defendant was guilty. Could the juror now be called in support of defendant's motion?

.6 *Donato v. Donato.* Gina's lawyer interviewed the children prior to trial. Richard indicated that, although he did not approve of his mother's relationship with Sam Gordon, Sam was always interested in Richard's activities and seemed to care about Allen and Ellen. At trial, however, Richard testifies that Sam always complains to Gina about the other kids, and that it seemed that he (Richard) could never do anything right when he and Sam were together. On cross-examination, by Mrs. Donato's lawyer, the following occurs:

> Q: Richard, you have been staying with your father for the week before this hearing, is that right?
>
> A: Yes.
>
> Q: In fact, he just bought you a car, didn't he?
>
> A: That's right.
>
> Q: Now Richard, you remember talking to me in my office two weeks ago?
>
> A: Yes.
>
> Q: We were alone, isn't that right?
>
> A: Yes.
>
> Q: At that time Richard, didn't you tell me that Sam had always been interested in Richard's activities and seemed to care for Allen and Ellen?
>
> A: No. I would never have said that.

When Mrs. Donato next has the opportunity to call witnesses, may her lawyer testify that Richard had indeed made the above statement to her in her office?

2.2 WITNESS INTERVIEW. *State v. Duffy.* You represent the defendant, Arlo Duffy. According to the police report, Roy Smith was a witness to the bank robbery. The police did not have Roy try to identify Arlo in the

lineup for reasons that follow. Roy, however, has been listed as a witness who will be testifying for the prosecution.

The police did not have Roy attempt an identification of Arlo, because Roy was not supposed to be in front of the bank when he was there. Roy is a resident of the state mental institution located in the city where the robbery occurred. Roy was involuntarily committed to the institution two years ago with a diagnosis of paranoid schizophrenia. This is the latest in a series of hospitalizations that began fifteen years ago. The recent commitment, instituted by his children, was precipitated by Roy's fear of being victimized by criminals. Roy had locked himself in his one bedroom apartment, literally nailing the door closed and boarding the windows. It took his children three days to convince Roy to let them enter the apartment. When they did enter, they found Roy curled in a corner of the room holding a gun and crying.

You have made an appointment to interview Roy in anticipation of trial. Your task is to gather as much information as you can concerning Roy's proposed testimony, and to evaluate Roy's competency to testify at trial. **Your instructor will provide the person playing Roy with confidential information. Be sure to fill out the joint questionnaire following the simulation.**

2.3 WITNESS INTERVIEW. *Donato v. Donato.* You are a law student clerking for the attorney that represents Mrs. Donato. Your supervising partner is considering having Allen Donato testify at the custody hearing concerning the events that occurred in Paul's apartment during the storm. One concern of your partner is whether Allen would be considered competent to testify. You have, therefore, been instructed to interview Allen. Your task is to gather as much information as you can concerning Allen's competency to testify. You have made an appointment to meet with Allen. Mrs. Donato has agreed to let you speak to him alone. **Your instructor will provide the person playing Allen with confidential information. Be sure to fill out the joint questionnaire following the simulation.**

2.4 Defendant is on trial for abduction and murder. The defendant files a pretrial motion to exclude the testimony of Tyrone Griffin, because hypnosis was used to refresh or attempt to refresh his memory. Griffin was apparently the last person to see the victim alive. He can testify, among other things, that he saw her get into a sports car approximately three hours before her body was found. At the hearing on the motion, it was established that a physician attempted to hypnotize Griffin. The physician then prompted Griffin to give a more detailed account of the day's events by intervening with questions as Griffin narrated the day's events. Police officers present during the hypnosis session testified that the physician's questions were not suggestive. The police also testified that the only new piece of information obtained during the session was the color of the car that Griffin saw the victim drive away in on the day of the alleged abduction. What result on defendant's motion? Suppose instead of attempting to hypnotize the witness before trial, the prosecutor seeks to have the witness hypnotized while on the witness stand. If defense counsel objects, what ruling?

2.5 *Paula v. David and PDG.* Assume that on cross-examination of Walter the following takes place:

> Q: Just before the accident, you were in the Triangle Tavern, weren't you?
>
> A: Yes.
>
> Q: You were there for an hour?
>
> A: About that.
>
> Q: You had four double vodkas, isn't that right?
>
> A: I wasn't counting.
>
> Q: You wouldn't deny that you had that many, would you?
>
> A: No, that sounds about right.
>
> Q: Your honor, at this point I move to strike the witness's testimony on direct examination on the basis that he did not have firsthand knowledge.

How should the judge rule?

2.6 On the issue of the location of a meeting, John Dean testifies that, "It was at the Mayflower Hotel, I think. I'm not positive, though. It could have been at the Shoreham which has a Mayflower restaurant."

2.7 Action in Tax Court, which under the Internal Revenue Code follows Federal Rule of Evidence 603. The standard oath used in the court states:

> I [witness name] do solemnly swear or affirm that the testimony I am about to give will be the truth, the whole truth, and nothing but the truth, so help me God.

The taxpayer calls a witness who, for religious reasons refuses to use the word "solemnly" in her oath. The Government objects to her testifying. What result? A second witness called by the taxpayer states "I can't take the oath if it has God's name in it. If you ask me if I'll tell the truth, I can say that." The Government objects to her testifying. What result? A third witness refuses to use the words "swear or affirm." The Government objects to her testifying. What result? A fourth witness refuses to take any oath at all. The judge asks her whether she will say, "I state that I will tell the truth in my testimony." She refuses. The Government objects to her testifying. What result?

2.8 In a criminal prosecution, the prosecutor seeks to introduce a tape of a telephone conversation. The conversation is completely in Spanish. The prosecutor, therefore, seeks to introduce a transcript of the tape that has been translated into English. The translator is called to the witness stand. What type of oath should be administered?

2.9   Defendant is on trial for conspiracy to distribute cocaine. The prosecution calls a witness William Earl McDonald. McDonald is sworn taking a standard oath that ends "so help me God." On cross-examination, McDonald admits he is an atheist. Defendant moves to strike McDonald's testimony. On questioning by the judge, McDonald then testifies that he took the oath seriously, that he respected the oath, and that "to the best of my ability, I'm telling the truth." What ruling on defendant's motion to strike?

Chapter 3

FORM OF THE QUESTION

3.1 DIRECT EXAMINATION. *State v. Duffy.* Arlo Duffy is on trial and the prosecutor has called Glenda Berg to the stand as the first witness. The following is a transcript of her testimony. Answer the questions associated with each objection.

[The witness was sworn]

Q: Would you tell us your name?

A: Glenda Berg.

Q: And where do you live?

A: 121 Elm St., here in Calhoun.

Q: How long have you lived there?

A: Five years.

Q: You work at First Investors on Main St. as a senior teller, is that right?

Defense Attorney: Objection, your honor, leading.

.1 State the correct ruling and the reason(s) for the ruling.

Q: How long have you worked there?

A: Four years, no actually three or three and a half.

Q: Directing your attention to June 1, Yr-0, at approximately 1:30 p.m., were you working?

Defense Attorney: Objection, your honor, leading

.2 State the correct ruling and the reason(s) for the ruling.

Q: Starting at the beginning and taking us step by step through the events, could you tell the jury what happened at approximately 1:30?

Defense Attorney: Objection, your honor.

.3 State the possible ground(s) for objection, the correct ruling, and the reason for the ruling.

A: I was working in the bank when a man came into the building.

Q: When did you first notice the defendant?

Defense Attorney: Objection, your honor.

.4 State the ground(s) for objection, the correct ruling, and the reason for the ruling.

> A: I first noticed him as he walked in the door.
>
> Q: About how far away from him were you?
>
> A: No more than thirty-five feet.
>
> Q: Why did you happen to notice him?
>
> A: Well there were no other customers in the bank at the time and he had this hat in his hands. Well, actually it was a ski cap, you know, one of those wool or knit things that pull over your head with holes for the eyes and nose.
>
> Q: Beginning from the point where you first noticed the man, tell us everything that happened?
>
> Defense Attorney: Objection, your honor.

.5 State the ground(s) for objection, the correct ruling, and the reason for the ruling.

> A: Well, I thought something was going to happen because he was carrying this hat and before I knew it he had pulled it over his head.
>
> Q: After he pulled the ski cap over his head, what happened?
>
> A: I immediately pressed the silent alarm and called Ms. Dodge.
>
> Q: Did the man go to your or Ms. Van Donk's window first?
>
> Defense Attorney: Objection, your honor.

.6 State the ground(s) for objection, the correct ruling, and the reason for the ruling.

> A: The man went to Sherry Van Donk's window first, and then came to mine.
>
> Q: Who is Ms. Van Donk?
>
> A: She is the other teller who was working in the bank on the day of the robbery?
>
> Q: Were you able to see and hear what he said to Ms. Van Donk?
>
> Defense Attorney: Objection, your honor.

.7 State the ground(s) for objection, the correct ruling, and the reason for the ruling.

> A: No, I just saw Sherry put money into his leather briefcase.
>
> Q: What happened then?
>
> Defense Attorney: Objection, your honor, assuming a fact not in evidence.

.8 State the correct ruling, and the reason for the ruling.

A: He came over to my window.

Q: And?

A: He pointed a big gun in my face.

Q: Did he say anything?

A: He didn't say anything, just pointed that big gun at me, and I gave him what money I had.

Q: What happened then?

A: He turned and ran away.

Q: Where did he run?

A: Out the door, back to Main Street.

Q: Now, Ms. Berg, you mentioned he had a gun. Was its barrel shiny like chrome, dark blue, or some other color?

Defense Attorney: Objection, your honor.

.9 State the ground(s) for objection, the correct ruling, and the reason for the ruling.

Q: Could you describe its barrel? Was it long or short?

Defense Attorney: Objection, your honor.

.10 State the ground(s) for objection, the correct ruling, and the reason for the ruling.

A: Long, maybe 6 inches.

Q: You also mentioned the briefcase. Could you describe it?

A: Yes. It was leather, a burgundy color. It looked like a hand sewn thing, you know, the kind you'd buy at a craft shop — real leather. It was maybe two inches thick and a rectangle, maybe 18 inches long and 12 inches wide. I think it closed with a buckle.

Q: Did it have a handle or did you carry it some other way?

Defense Attorney: Objection, your honor.

.11 State the ground(s) for objection, the correct ruling, and the reason for the ruling.

A: It had a handle, a strap about one inch wide and maybe eight inches long.

Q: Are you able to describe the robber?

A: He was a white guy, I'd say in his late twenties, but that's just a guess. You know his shape made him look on the young side. He was maybe 5'9" or so and 160 lbs.

Q: Excuse me, was that 5'9"?

Defense Attorney: Objection, your honor.

.12 State the ground(s) for objection, the correct ruling, and the reason for the ruling.

Q: You testified earlier that he came right up to your window; so you had a pretty good view of him?

Defense Attorney: Objection, your honor.

.13 State the ground(s) for objection, the correct ruling, and the reason for the ruling.

Q: I have no further questions, thank you.

3.2 *Paula v. David and PDG.* May Paula call David as a witness and ask, "Isn't it true that on January 15, of last year, at approximately 4:15 p.m., you were driving a truck owned by the defendant?", and "You were on company business at the time weren't you?"

3.3 Defendant is on trial for shoplifting a watch. On direct examination, the prosecutor calls as a witness the companion of the defendant on the day of the alleged shoplifting. The prosecutor asks the question, "Isn't it true that you saw the defendant place the gold watch in his pocket?" Defendant objects. What ruling and why? Assume the witness had previously refused to speak to the prosecutor. Would that affect your answer?

3.4 Assume that the questions in 3.2 were allowed, and that the plaintiff's lawyer did not ask any additional questions. On cross-examination, David's lawyer asks the following questions. Should they be permitted over a timely objection?

Q: Isn't it true that you normally get off work at 3:30?

Q: You've lived and worked in this city for 10 years, haven't you?

Q: Plaintiff hit you, didn't she?

Q: You didn't see plaintiff before she struck you, did you?

Q: Was plaintiff in the intersection when you struck her?

3.5 LAW PROFESSOR ARRESTED FOR ROBBERY. Your client is your evidence professor. He or she is charged with driving the get-away car in an armed robbery of a bank at the corner of Main and Third Streets at 3:00 p.m. August 26, Yr — 0. As the professor's lawyer, you should attempt to elicit all the information contained in this statement. All students not doing the direct examination should object to all improperly formed questions, being prepared to state the reason for the objection.

* * *

My name is _____ and I live at _____. I am employed
as a Professor at _____ Law School. On August 26, Yr-0, I was
so employed and arrived at the law school at approximately 7:30 a.m. The
reason I was late was that I had received a long distance phone call at
home from an old professor of mine who needed help preparing for his
class. I went immediately to my office to prepare for evidence.

At 9:00 a.m., I received a call from the director of the local legal services
office concerning a proposed training conference. We arranged a meeting for 1:45 at my office. At 10:00 I went to the other class I teach besides
evidence and taught until 10:50. Students had lots of questions after
class so I did not get back to my office until 12:00 noon. I stayed in my
office until 2:00 p.m., when the director of legal services showed up
(fifteen minutes late). We talked for fifteen minutes and then went to
lunch at the Peking Restaurant at the corner of Main and Third Streets.
I drove my car, a blue Toyota. The Peking is located just diagonally
across from the bank that was apparently robbed. At about 3:15, we
finished lunch and as we left the restaurant, I heard sirens and saw a
blue subcompact car go speeding by me on Third Street. Its license
number was XYZ 999.

At 3:30 p.m., I returned to my office to prepare for the next day's
evidence class. At 4:30 I had coffee with Professor _____ in her
office. At 5:00 I returned to my office to work on my evidence treatise. I
stayed in my office until 8:00 p.m. I had to leave early that night to go to
a social gathering of faculty in the faculty lounge celebrating the
beginning of a new academic year. I stayed there until about 10:00 p.m.,
and then went home.

At 11:00 p.m., while I was reviewing the galleys of my most recent
article, the police knocked on my door and arrested me for robbing a
bank on Main at Third. I don't know anything about any robbery. That
is the truth.

/s/ <u>Professor</u>

3.6　*State v. Duffy.* Prepare the direct examination of Sherry Van Donk. Be
sure to establish her credibility, set the scene to which she will testify and elicit
a narrative of her testimony. It is also usually wise to elicit any unfavorable
testimony rather than waiting until the cross-examiner brings it out.

3.7　Refer to problem 3.5. Assume the professor cannot remember the color of
the subcompact car. Refresh his or her recollection using the statement to the
police. How else might you refresh his or her recollection?

3.8   *Paula v. David and PDG.* During Paula's deposition, the following occurs:

> Q: All right. Without disclosing the contents of any discussions you had with your attorney, how did you prepare for this deposition,?
>
> A: I looked over some notes that I had been keeping?
>
> Q: When you say "notes," what notes are you referring to?
>
> A: Notes that I gave to my attorney.
>
> Q: Were these handwritten notes?
>
> A: Yes.
>
> Q: When did you make these notes?
>
> A: Just after the accident.
>
> Q: Before you hired a lawyer?
>
> A: Yes sir.

Defense counsel files a pre-trial motion seeking discovery of the notes. What result?

Chapter 4

HEARSAY

A. The Hearsay Rule

4.1 THE BASIC CONCEPT. For each of the following, indicate whether the evidence is hearsay.

.1 *Paula v. David and PDG.* On the issue of whether the light was green for David, the witness will testify that Walter told him the light was green for David.

.2 *Paula v. David and PDG.* On the issue of whether the light was green for David, David seeks to introduce a portion of Walter's deposition in which Walter stated that the light was green for David.

.3 *State v. Duffy.* On the issue of how many people were in the bank at the time of the robbery, Officer Gorham will testify that Sherry Van Donk told him that there were five customers in the bank.

.4 In an action to quiet title, the plaintiff seeks to introduce testimony that he told a group of teenagers, "I own this property, now get off."

.5 In an action for defamation, brought by a priest, the defendant is alleged to have said that the priest frequents a house of prostitution. Defendant wishes to introduce evidence that the priest's reputation in the community is that he is unchaste.

.6 *State v. Duffy.* On the issue of how many people were in the bank at the time of the robbery, Sherry Van Donk will testify that she told Officer Gorham that there were five customers in the bank.

.7 On the issue of whether Charlie was one of a group of boys who were at a party on Tuesday night, the high school principal will testify, "I went to Charlie's classroom on Wednesday morning and asked the entire class, who was at the party Tuesday night? Charlie raised his hand."

.8 On the issue of whether Charlie did not like Charlotte, Harold will testify that Charlie told him that he hated Charlotte.

.9 On the issue of whether Charlie did not like Charlotte, Harold will testify that Charlie told him that he, Charlie, thought Charlotte was a liar.

.10 *State v. Duffy.* On the issue of whether there were gunshots associated with the robbery, defense counsel seeks to have a private investigator testify that he talked to people in the bank, and in businesses close by, and that no one heard any gunshots.

.11 Plaintiff brought suit challenging the constitutionality of a federal statute that limits the amount of money political committees may spend to support candidates for office. To establish the government's interest in passing the statute, the government seeks to introduce a magazine article that reported several people interviewed in Washington, D.C., said that numerous top officials in the executive branch got their jobs by making significant contributions to political campaigns.

.12 On the issue of whether the parties entered into a contract, the plaintiff seeks to introduce testimony that he told the defendant, "That sounds great, I'll take all the widgets you've got at your price of $25 each."

.13 Former friends dispute the ownership of an antique gun. Ben claims the gun was a gift from Al. Al claims he merely let Ben borrow the gun and now wants it back. The gun, Al claims, was a family heirloom given to him by his father. Ben will testify Al came to his house and, handing the gun to Ben said, "You've been a good friend. Here I want you to have this."

.14 In a criminal prosecution for income tax evasion, defendant wishes to testify that she was told by her accountant that it was proper to take certain deductions.

.15 Defendant, a convicted felon, is charged with illegal possession of a firearm. Defendant was arrested during a lawful search of his father's house. Defendant was holding the gun at the time of his arrest. One element of the crime is that defendant was not justified in possessing the firearm. Defendant claims that the gun is his father's. He claims he only picked it up because he thought the police were really a neighborhood gang breaking into his father's house. To rebut this claim, the prosecutor wishes to introduce testimony of a police officer who will say, "I was at the back door of the house, in order to keep anyone from fleeing. Officer Smith was in the front of the house. At 8:30 a.m. sharp, I heard Officer Smith yell, 'This is the police. Open up!'"

.16 In the previous problem, assume defendant did not have the gun in his hand. During the search of the house, the police found a holster and gun in a dresser which defendant admits is where he keeps his clothes. The holster has initials inscribed on it that are the same as the defendant's. On the issue of whether the defendant possessed the gun, the prosecutor seeks to introduce the holster and gun.

.17 ***Paula v. David and PDG.*** To prove what time the accident occurred, Walter seeks to testify that the clock on the nearby bank indicated that it was 1:00 p.m.

.18 ***Paula v. David and PDG.*** To prove what time the accident occurred, Walter seeks to testify that the clock in the nearby church tower chimed once, indicating that it was 1:00 p.m.

.19 *Paula v. David and PDG.* To prove what time the accident occurred, Walter seeks to testify that he thought the time might be important, so as a soon as he saw the accident, he stopped his watch. Later that day he looked at it and it was stopped at 1:00 p.m.

.20 To prove that one bid on a government contract was received before another, a party seeks to introduce the two bids, each of which was stamped by a secretary using an automatic time and date machine.

4.2   A BIT MORE COMPLICATED. For each of the following, indicate whether the evidence is hearsay.

.1 In a criminal prosecution for homicide, the defendant, Harry, asserts a claim of self-defense and seeks to introduce testimony that the victim had a reputation in the community as a violent person. Further, Harry seeks to have a witness testify that he, the witness, heard the victim tell a group of people, "Harry's a dead man. I'm out to get him."

.2 *State v. Duffy.* On the issue of whether Arlo Duffy believes he is guilty, Roy Smith will testify that at the time the robbery was taking place, he saw Arlo running away from the bank.

.3 In a murder prosecution, a police officer proposes to testify that the day after the murder he went to the defendant's house and asked the defendant's mother to give him the clothes defendant wore the previous day. The mother gave the officer a set of clothing. The prosecutor seeks to have the clothes introduced.

.4 Plaintiff, a physician, sues defendant insurance company on the theory of bad faith failure to settle within the policy limits of the plaintiff's medical malpractice insurance coverage. Plaintiff seeks to introduce a letter from her to the insurance company in which she stated, "I am in receipt of your letter indicating that my former patient Mr. Smith is willing to settle this matter for $500,000. This is well within my policy limits and I hereby give you notice that you should accept his offer to settle."

4.3   WHAT'S THE PROPOSITION? For each of the following, indicate if the evidence is hearsay.

.1 *Paula v. David and PDG.* Walter testifies on direct examination that David had the green light. On cross-examination, Brewster asks, "Isn't it true that immediately after the accident you told the police officer the light was red for the defendant?"

.2 *State v. Duffy.* Officer Gorham will testify that when he approached Arlo, then a suspect in the criminal investigation, and asked his name, Arlo responded, "Al Smith."

.3 Defendant is charged with mail fraud and asserts as a defense lack of intent. The prosecutor seeks to introduce evidence of complaints of mail fraud to the Better Business Bureau made by customers of the defendant over the course of several years.

.4 Plaintiff brings an action against an airline and an airplane manufacturer arising out of an airplane crash. The accident was allegedly caused by an explosion resulting from a leaking fuel line. Plaintiff seeks to introduce the flight checklist of the pilot in which the pilot indicated that the fuel line had a leak.

.5 In the previous problem, Plaintiff also seeks to introduce the testimony of a janitor working at the airport who will testify that he heard a mechanic tell the pilot, "the fuel line has a leak," and the pilot responded, "That's okay, it's something in the way they designed the stupid thing. It always leaks a bit."

.6 In a prosecution for perjury, the prosecutor seeks to introduce the grand jury transcript containing the statement alleged to constitute perjury.

.7 In problem 4.1.5, plaintiff seeks to introduce the testimony of Walker who, if allowed, will testify that he heard the defendant say that the plaintiff was unchaste.

.8 In the previous problem, plaintiff seeks to introduce the testimony of Walker who, if allowed, will testify that he heard Debra say that the defendant said that the plaintiff was unchaste.

.9 Assume that in the previous problem, plaintiff is suing both the original defendant and Debra.

4.4 SOME PROBLEM AREAS. For each of the following indicate whether the evidence is hearsay.

.1 A man, Max Klinger, in order to get a psychiatric discharge from the army, needs to prove that he is insane. Max wants to introduce testimony from a witness who will testify that Max always goes around saying "I'm a woman, and I shouldn't be in the Army." Max also wants to introduce testimony from a witness who will testify that Max always wears dresses. Finally, Max wishes to introduce testimony from a witness who will state, "Max comes to talk to me. He is very concerned about whether he should adopt, since he was having trouble getting pregnant."

.2 *State v. Duffy.* The prosecutor offers a police investigator who will testify that when questioned, Arlo's mother indicated that Arlo was with her on the day of the robbery. The investigator, however, will also say he has a videotape of Arlo at a party at his apartment on the day of the robbery.

B. Prior Statements

4.5 Defendant is charged with violation of the immigration laws by aiding several foreign nationals in attempts to enter the country illegally. The aliens, driving a van registered in defendant's name, were apprehended by the Border Patrol and taken to the Patrol's station house. The aliens then made tape recorded, sworn statements implicating the defendant in their illegal entry. At trial, the aliens denied that defendant was involved in the illegal entry. Are the statements made to the Border Patrol admissible under Federal Rule 801(d)(1)(A)? Can these statements be distinguished from statements made by witnesses to police officers at a station house? Is there any additional information you would like to know?

4.6   *Paula v. David and PDG.* On direct examination, Wanda testifies that David was speeding just before the accident. On cross-examination, Wanda is asked:

> Q: Didn't you tell the police on the day of the accident that David was driving at the speed limit?

> A: Yes.

> Q: Isn't it true that you began dating the plaintiff two weeks ago?

> A: Yes.

On redirect, the witness is asked:

> Q: Have you ever told anyone else how fast David was driving at the time of the accident?

> A: Yes.

> Q: When was this?

> A: About four weeks ago.

> Q: Whom did you tell this to?

> A: You, when came to my house and asked me some questions.

> Q: What did you tell me?

Defense counsel then objected. Paula's counsel makes an offer of proof that, if allowed to testify, the witness will state, "As I explained to you then, I had gotten mixed up at the accident scene about whose car was whose, and made a mistake. I told you David was speeding." How should the judge rule? Assume the conversation with the lawyer occurred just one week ago. What ruling?

4.7   Defendant, already convicted and serving time in prison on another charge, was indicted for possession of marijuana. An element the prosecutor needs to establish is that the defendant was aware of the marijuana that was found in his locker in the prison dormitory. A corrections officer, Castello, testified that after the marijuana was found, he took the defendant to a different cell and on the way there the defendant stated, "Alright, you got me now. Tell me who fingered me." On cross-examination of Castello, the following occurred:

> Q: Officer Castello, you wrote a report of this incident didn't you?

A: Yes.

Q: That's the same report you referred to on direct examination?

A: Yes

Q: Could you point out where in that report it says the defendant made the statement, "Tell me who fingered me?"

A: That statement is not in the report.

The government then calls a second corrections officer who testifies that on the day the drugs were seized he had been told by officer Castello that the defendant said, "Tell me who fingered me." Defense counsel objects. What is the proper ruling?

4.8 Doug is charged with the rape of Alice. Alice is the nine-year-old daughter of Doug's girlfriend. On direct examination, Alice testifies that Doug raped her. On cross-examination of Alice, defense counsel asks:

Q: You visit your Daddy a lot, don't you Alice?

A: Yes.

Q: You like going to visit him?

A: Yes.

Q: Now, I know this may be hard for you to say in front of everybody, but it's important. You would prefer to live with your Daddy wouldn't you?

A: I love my mommy.

In rebuttal, the prosecutor seeks to call Mary who, if allowed, will testify that after the defendant was indicted, but before trial, Alice told her (Mary) that Doug raped her (Alice).

4.9 *State v. Duffy.*

.1 Sherry Van Donk takes the witness stand and testifies, "I went down to the police station and saw a bunch of guys in, I guess, what they call a lineup and I told them that it was that guy Duffy that robbed the bank." Is this admissible?

.2 Assume instead of the teller, a police offer takes that stand and says, "Ms. Van Donk came to the station to view a lineup and she said that Arlo Duffy was the one who robbed the bank." Is this admissible?

.3 Assume that Ms. Van Donk denies ever having identified Arlo Duffy as the robber. May the police officer testify as in the previous question?

.4 The prosecutor calls a police officer to the stand to introduce a letter purportedly signed by Harold Johnson that states that the writer was standing at his window when he saw Arlo run out of the bank carrying a brief case.

.5 Arlo has brown eyes. On cross-examination, Sherry Van Donk testifies that she does not remember the color of the robber's eyes. On cross-examination, Officer Mundy is asked by defense counsel, "Isn't it true that Ms. Van Donk told you that the robber's eyes were blue?" The prosecutor objects, what ruling?

C. Admissions

4.10   For each of the following, indicate whether the evidence is hearsay under the Federal Rules of Evidence or at common law. If it is hearsay at common law, is it admissible as an admission of a party opponent?

.1 Plaintiff, in a suit involving an intersection collision, is alleged to have negligently entrusted his automobile to his daughter. Defendant wishes to introduce the testimony of Denise who will state that she overheard plaintiff tell his neighbor, "I don't know what to do with my daughter. She is just so reckless in the car."

.2 Refer to problem 4.1.13. Al seeks to call Walter who will testify that he, Walter, went hunting with Ben and Ben told him that "Al's great, he's letting me use this antique gun."

.3 Reconsider 4.2.2.

.4 Defendants Nash and Coco are on trial for violation of anti-loan sharking laws and the murder of Victor. The prosecutor calls Walter to the stand to testify that he, Walter, asked Nash and Coco whatever happened to Victor. Walter will testify that Nash said, "He fell into the canal — no one cared," and that Coco "just smiled."

.5 *Paula v. David and PDG.* Paula initially alleged in her complaint that the weather was cold and raining. Later, pursuant to a provision similar to Federal Rule of Civil Procedure 15, Paula amended her complaint to allege that the weather was clear and dry. As required under local procedural rules, Paula signed the complaint. Defendants seek to introduce into evidence the superseded complaint.

.6 *Paula v. David and PDG.* Assume Paula first sued David and PDG alleging in the complaint that the weather was cold and raining. As required under local procedural rules, Paula signed the complaint. Paula subsequently sued Walter, alleging that the weather was clear and dry. Walter seeks to introduce the complaint filed in the suit against David and PDG.

.7 Plaintiff sued defendant in a civil action for assault and battery. Plaintiff wishes to introduce the guilty plea defendant entered in a criminal assault and battery action arising out of the same actions causing plaintiff to bring her suit.

4.11 *Paula v. David and PDG.* Paula claims a back injury resulting from the accident. Defendants contend the back injury was a preexisting condition, and seek to introduce a health form attached to Paula's application for college. The form, signed by a physician two years ago, indicates an abnormal back. Paula objects to the introduction of the form. What ruling? Assume that instead of being attached to an application for college, the form was filled out by a physician as part of Paula's application for a summer job in a factory. Paula objects to the introduction of the form. What ruling?

4.12 In a consumer fraud action involving allegations of bait and switch, plaintiff seeks to introduce evidence that he went to the defendant's store during business hours. He said to the store owner, within hearing of several other customers, "You guys think you're pretty smart. You advertise that cheap stuff and then never have it when the customer comes in." The defendant made no response. Is plaintiff's testimony admissible?

4.13 *Paula v. David and PDG.* David does not take the stand, nor does he offer any eyewitness testimony. Instead, David chooses to rely on accident reconstruction experts. In closing argument, Paula's attorney argues, "It seems strange that the defendant did not take the stand on his own behalf." Is this argument objectionable?

4.14 Consider:

.1 Assume in problem 4.10.6 that instead of the Paula signing the complaint, the complaint was signed by the Paula's lawyer. Is the complaint admissible?

.2 *State v. Duffy.* Arlo seeks to call a newspaper reporter who will testify that Officer Gorham said during the investigation, "I never have thought Arlo was smart enough to pull off this job." Is the testimony admissible?

4.15 Plaintiff claims that a truck driver while on company business struck the plaintiff as she walked across a parking lot.

.1 Immediately upon hitting the plaintiff, the truck driver got out of the truck and said, "Gee, I'm sorry. I didn't see you." In the suit against the employer based on respondeat superior, may plaintiff testify to the driver's statement?

.2 Assume that instead of making the statement immediately after the accident, the driver visited the plaintiff in the hospital that evening and made the statement. Would there be a different result?

.3 Assume that between the time the accident occurred, and the time the driver went to the hospital to make the statement, the employer fired the truck driver. Would that change your answer in 4.15.2?

.4 Would the fact that the driver was fired on the day of the accident be admissible? Suppose at the time the truck driver was fired the employer said, "I'm tired of your carelessness, you're fired." Could the employee's statement be testified to by the driver?

4.16   In a wrongful death action, an airline is sued for negligence when a plane crashed on landing. Before the lawsuit was filed, an employee of the airline, an engineering test pilot, conducted an investigation of the accident. When contacted by the plaintiff after suit was filed, the employee wrote a letter to the plaintiff stating, "The consensus is that this was an unfortunate accident, just too short and low a landing." Defendant objects to the admissibility of this letter based on hearsay. Should the letter be excluded? Would your answer be different if the quoted statement were contained in an internal report resulting from an investigation authorized by the company and conducted by the employee? Would it make any difference if the pilot made the statement on the basis of only having talked to two eyewitnesses?

4.17   Plaintiff sues the owner of a grocery store for negligence in not mopping up a spill on the floor. Plaintiff alleges she slipped and fell on the spill and suffered injury. A clerk, seeing the plaintiff fall came up to her and said, "Sorry the floor was wet, I was just getting ready to mop it up." May plaintiff testify to the clerk's statement over an objection of hearsay? Assume it was the store manager that made the statement, what result?

4.18   Robert Chappell is charged with a scheme to defraud investors in an oil well. Criminal charges were filed after a Securities Exchange Commission (SEC) investigation. At trial, the prosecutor seeks to introduce the transcript of the deposition of a former employee of Chappell's. The employee was the bookkeeper employed by Chappell during the time of the SEC investigation. The deposition was taken in conjunction with the SEC investigation. The bookkeeper left the company one year ago, but remains as bookkeeper in an independent contractor status. The former employee is available to testify. Is the deposition admissible?

4.19   Refer to problem 4.16. Assume the airline is the wholly owned subsidiary of a larger diversified corporation. Assume also that the letter came not from the airline company actually involved in the accident, but from the parent corporation of the airline. Under what circumstances, if any, should the letter be admissible by plaintiff?

4.20   Refer to problems 4.1.13. Suppose Al wins and is then sued by Oscar. Oscar claims that he, not Al, is the true owner of the gun. Oscar wishes to introduce the testimony of a neighbor of Al's now deceased father who will testify that Al's father said to the neighbor, "I took that sucker [meaning the antique gun] from Oscar's daddy and he didn't even know, ha ha." Al objects. What ruling?

4.21 Defendant is on trial for possession of drugs. Defendant was arrested with two other people, Carol and Gary, when the Coast Guard boarded a boat based on probable cause to believe the defendant and the other two planned to smuggle drugs. After the boat was taken into custody, it was searched and its contents catalogued.

.1 The prosecutor seeks to introduce the testimony of a Coast Guard officer. The officer will testify that after he boarded the boat, but before he began to search, one of defendant's companions said, that the boat was a charter operation taking scuba divers out to the reef, and "we are all in this together." Defendant objects to the testimony on the basis of hearsay. What ruling? Does it make a difference whether the companion is unavailable?

.2 Assume the quoted portion of the statement was made after the drugs were found and during questioning in which the declarant admitted his guilt on drug charges. What result?

.3 Assume the statement was made in the presence of the defendant and that the defendant remained silent. What result?

.4 A cellular phone was found on the boat. Carol identified the phone as one given to her for use during the trip. A day or two after the arrest, the phone rang and the Coast Guard officer answered it. During the conversation, which was not recorded, the caller asked "where the girl or Gary was." Realizing the caller was asking about the people arrested on the boat, the officer quickly ended the conversation and set up equipment to record subsequent calls. There was one subsequent phone call that was recorded. Carol later identified the recorded voice of the caller as that of the "fat guy" who had provided her money to rent the boat, purchased the cellular phone for her, and called her on the phone during the trip. Defendant objects to the Coast Guard officer testifying to the substance of the first phone call as hearsay. What result?

.5 A nautical chart was also found on the boat. The chart has pencil markings apparently indicating the route the defendant had taken on the boat. Defendant objects to introducing the chart. What result?

4.22 Fred Potter unsuccessfully ran against Stewart Jones in an election for a local trial court. Phoebe Potter, Fred's daughter, brings suit under 42 U.S.C.A. § 1983 claiming that during the election Lee Davis, a psychologist employed by the Family Court, conspired with others to release confidential juvenile court records. Specifically, Phoebe alleges that Davis, a political supporter of Jones', conspired to disclose Phoebe's confidential psychological records in an effort to hurt her father's campaign.

Phoebe's only evidence that Davis disclosed the records originates from Wenona Franklin, a local radio personality. Franklin informed Phoebe's father that information about his daughter's juvenile counseling records was being circulated by Jones. Phoebe's father Fred arranged with Wenona to telephone Jones while Fred was listening, without Jones's knowing Fred was listening.

Fred and Wenona are prepared to testify that during this conversation, Jones disclosed information from Phoebe's counseling records and stated that "I learned about Phoebe's records from Lee Davis." Defense counsel objects to the introduction Fred's and Wenona's testimony. What ruling?

4.23 Defendants Henry and Harrison are charged with drug conspiracy and intent to distribute heroin. It is alleged that they conspired with Lama, a Nepalese national. It is alleged that under the arrangement between Lama and the defendants, Lama imported the drugs and then sold them to defendants who in turn distributed the drugs. The government seeks to introduce a videotape of its agent, Bryant that purports to show Bryant and Lama engaging in drug deals and negotiating future drug deals. The videotape was taken during the time that the conspiracy is alleged to have been conducted. The only evidence connecting Lama and the defendants is evidence that Lama eventually sold the drugs in the videotape to Henry and Harrison. Defendants object to the evidence based on relevancy and hearsay. What result?

D. Spontaneous Declarations

4.24 Defendant, an air-conditioning repair technician, is charged with murder. The prosecutor calls to the stand the husband of the victim who, if allowed, will testify that 30 minutes before his wife was found dead, he talked to his wife on the phone and she said,

.1 "I haven't been able to get to the store yet, since the guy is still here repairing the air conditioner."

.2 "I still can't get to the store, the air-conditioning guy left fifteen minutes ago, I hope to get a part. At least I think he's coming back."

Is this testimony admissible over hearsay objections?

4.25 *Donato v. Donato.* Paul calls to the witness stand a neighbor of Gina's who will testify that she was walking past Gina's house when a person she had never seen before, but believes was a salesman, came out of the house and said, "What a pig sty. I can't believe people actually live in that mess." Is this testimony admissible over a hearsay objection?

4.26 Refer to problem 4.15. The truck driver after hitting the plaintiff got out of the truck and said, "I'm in big trouble now. My boss told me to get this load delivered by quitting time." May plaintiff testify over a hearsay objection that this statement was made?

4.27 Defendant decided to go joyriding in a rented car accompanied by his friend and a gun. Defendant was tried and convicted on a charge of felon in possession of a firearm. Defendant appealed claiming the trial court improperly allowed introduction of the following evidence. Pam testified that she was walking with her teenage cousin and two small children when she saw a man she recognized as the defendant riding in a vehicle, and was able to see that he was holding a gun. Pam testified that she was alarmed for two reasons: because she saw the gun and because she thought defendant had been involved in a murder that occurred about a week earlier at the Brick House. Pam felt responsible for the safety of the small children and picked up her pace. She immediately called 911, but her initial 911 call was dropped. When she called back and was reconnected, she recited the license plate number she saw as BEW 7533, and said that the car was a Ford Focus. She also told the dispatcher it had been five minutes since she saw him, but she testified that this was incorrect and it had only been between thirty seconds and a minute. How should the appellate court rule?

4.28   Refer to problem 4.8. Forty-five minutes after the alleged rape, Alice was taken by her grandmother to the police. Alice testifies first. The prosecutor then calls a police officer who, if allowed, will testify as follows:

Q: What did you do when the grandmother brought in the girl?

A: Well, the first thing I noticed was her clothes were all torn and her face was beginning to show some bruises, so I asked, 'What happened?'

Q: How did Alice respond?

A: She immediately broke down and started to cry, but then kind of between sobs she tells me that her Mommy's friend, the defendant there, tried to pull down her jeans, and tried to touch her places her mommy told her not to let people. When she fought and screamed, she said the defendant hit her.

Is this testimony admissible?

4.29   The State charged Davis with felony violation of domestic battery and of a domestic no-contact order. On the night of the alleged assault, the victim made a 911 call to the police. A police officer testified that she and her partner arrived at the victim's house within four minutes of the 911 call and observed the victim's shaken state, "fresh injuries on her forearm and her face," and her "frantic efforts to gather her belongings and her children so that they could leave the residence." The victim has refused to testify against Davis.

.1 At trial, the prosecutor seeks to introduce the following transcript of the 911 call made by the victim. Defense counsel objects. How should the court rule?

911 Operator: Hello.

Complainant: Hello.

911 Operator: What's going on?

Complainant: He's here jumping on me again.

911 Operator: Okay. Listen to me carefully. Are you in a house or an apartment?

Complainant: I'm in a house.

911 Operator: Are there any weapons?

Complainant: No. He's using his fists.

911 Operator: Okay. Has he been drinking?

Complainant: No.

911 Operator: Okay, sweetie. I've got help started. Stay on the line with me, okay?

Complainant: I'm on the line.

911 Operator: Listen to me carefully. Do you know his last name?

Complainant: It's Davis.

911 Operator: Davis? Okay, what's his first name?

Complainant: Adrian

911 Operator: What is it?

Complainant: Adrian.

911 Operator: Adrian?

Complainant: Yeah.

911 Operator: Okay. What's his middle name?

Complainant: Martell. He's running now.

.2 After arriving at the scene the officers searched the house to determine that Davis had fled the scene. The officers then questioned the victim. After hearing her account, the officer had her fill out and sign a battery affidavit. The victim handwrote the following: "Broke our Furnace & shoved me down on the floor into the broken glass. Hit me in the chest and threw me down. Broke our lamps & phone. Tore up my van where I couldn't leave the house. Attacked my daughter." The prosecution seeks to introduce the affidavit. Defense counsel objects. How should the court rule?

4.30   Danny is on trial for robbery of a liquor store that he is alleged to have robbed with his friend Joe. Joe has already been convicted of the crime. Immediately after fleeing the scene of the crime, it is alleged that Danny and Joe went to Joe's girlfriend's house and partied through the night. At various times during the night Danny left the party. As the party was winding down, Joe started to count his money taken in the robbery and the girlfriend asked, "Where's Danny's share?" Joe replied, "He has already gone through all of his money." The prosecutor seeks to call the girlfriend to testify to this exchange with Joe. Defense counsel objects. What result?

4.31   Sarah, the owner of a wine distributorship, sues Betty, the owner of a wine shop, for breach of contract. Sarah claims that she and Betty contracted for the purchase of several cases of expensive French wine. Sarah claims her copy of the correspondence that forms the contract has been destroyed in a recent fire. Betty denies the existence of the contract. Is the following testimony hearsay, and if so, is it admissible under Federal Rule of Evidence 803(3) or its common law equivalent?

.1 Sarah will testify that in a letter from her to Betty she offered to sell the wine for $5,000, and that a letter in response stated that Betty would buy it for $4,000. Sarah then sent a letter saying she would sell the wine for $4,000.

.2 Sarah will call Warren, the owner of a different wine shop. Warren will testify that a day before Sarah allegedly sent her original letter to Betty, he was at Sarah's warehouse and offered to buy the wine. Sarah refused his offer, saying, "No, I want to see this in Betty's shop. Her customers will appreciate it."

.3 Suppose Warren will testify that just before Sarah sent the letter agreeing to the $4,000, Warren was at Sarah's warehouse. Warren saw the wine in question and offered to buy it. Sarah, however, refused to sell it, saying, "No, I'm going to sell that to your competitor, Betty, and I'm getting four grand."

.4 Suppose Warren visited the warehouse after Sarah allegedly sent the letter accepting the $4,000 counter offer. When Warren asked to purchase the wine, Sarah said, "Sorry, you're too late. I've sold it to your competitor, Betty."

4.32   Defendant is charged with extortion. The prosecutor claims the defendant came into possession of credit card invoices and then made extortionate demands for their return. Defendant seeks to introduce the testimony of his previous lawyer who will state that at some point prior to defendant's arrest he and the defendant discussed the legality of the defendant negotiating a reward for having found credit card invoices. Specifically, the lawyer will testify that the defendant said, "I intend to negotiate a reward. Is it legal?" Is the testimony admissible? Suppose, instead, the lawyer will testify that the defendant said, "Is it legal to negotiate for a reward for something you find?" Are these statements admissible? Would it make a difference what the lawyer said in response? Is what the lawyer said hearsay?

4.33   Refer to problem 4.24. The victim's husband will testify as follows.

.1 "I spoke to Mary about 30 minutes before the neighbor found her dead. She called me from the store to tell me she was running home because she had to meet the air conditioner repairman."

.2 "I spoke with Mary about 30 minutes before the neighbor found her dead. She called me from home and said she had run home from the store to meet the repairman, but that he was late."

Defendant's attorney objects. What ruling?

4.34 Defendant is charged with raping Alice, a nine-year-old. When her grandmother discovered Alice shaking and crying in her bedroom, she called the police. After talking to the police, Alice was taken by the police and her grandmother to the hospital emergency room where she was seen by a physician, Dr. Harris. The prosecutor seeks to call Dr. Harris who, if allowed, will testify as follows:

> I came into the room and I asked Alice what happened. She did not answer. I asked her if she had any pain and she pointed to her vaginal area. I then asked her if she hurt anyplace else, but she did not answer. I asked again what happened and she said Doug had dragged her to her bedroom. I asked if he had taken off her clothes and she said yes. Then she said that he had tried to stick something into her vagina which hurt. She tried to scream, but was unable, because Doug had a hand over her mouth and neck.

.1 Is this testimony admissible under Federal Rule 803(4) over defense counsel's objection?

.2 Assume that Dr. Harris was unable to get any information from Alice, and turned to the police officer who had interviewed her. The police officer then told Dr. Harris that on the car ride over, Alice had told him this information. May Dr. Harris testify over defense counsel's objection concerning what the police officer told him?

.3 Assume Dr. Harris is a psychiatrist. Also assume Alice is four years old, rather than nine, and was taken to Dr. Harris' office in a suburban building and introduced to Alice as a friend of Alice's grandmother. Is this testimony admissible under Federal Rule 803(4) over defense counsel's objection?

4.35 Adam Klare brought suit for medical malpractice against Donald Bradman, a physician. Bradman allegedly failed to come to the hospital when Adam needed his attention. Bradman is the only defendant. Bradman admitted Adam to the hospital for an operation to repair a broken leg. One night at the hospital, at approximately 3:00 a.m., Adam complained of pain in the leg and lack of feeling in his toes. The toes were cold and bluish in color. These were all indications that the cast was cutting off the circulation in his lower leg. The nurse assigned to Adam's room that night was Diane Loso. Bradman's defense is that he was never informed of the seriousness of the symptoms.

For each of the following indicate whether the evidence is hearsay and if so whether it is admissible under an exception to the hearsay rule.

.1 Adam seeks to have his mother take the stand to testify that Adam called her at about 3:10 a.m. and told her, "My leg hurts something awful, and the doctor's don't seem to care. It's turning bluer and bluer because the doctors won't take care of it. What should I do?" His mother will also testify that she called the hospital after talking to her son, and told the nurses that her son was in great pain.

.2 Adam seeks to call Diane Loso to testify that he (Adam) said at 3:00 a.m., "My leg started hurting an hour ago, and it hurts somethin' awful right now."

.3 Adam seeks to take the stand himself to testify that at approximately 3:20 a.m., nurse Loso came to his room and said, "Don't worry, I've spoken to Dr. Bradman, and he said that everything would be fine and that he'll see you in the morning."

.4 Bradman seeks to call a second nurse, Candice Krieling, to testify that Loso said at approximately 3:15 a.m., "I'm going to call Bradman. Klare's in there complaining again. It's always something with that guy."

.5 Joe Basanta was in the bed next to Adam on the night in question. Joe also had a broken leg. Six months after the night in question, Joe was in a car crash and suffered injuries which ultimately caused his death. Before he died, however, Joe was taken back to the same hospital in which the present malpractice is alleged to have occurred. As Joe lay dying in the same hospital with two severed legs caused by the car crash, the only words he said were, "Don't let them take me back to the same floor I was on before. Those nurses cost Adam his leg." Adam wishes to call Gene Basanta, Joe's father, who was present at the time Joe made this statement.

E. Records

4.36 WITNESS EXAMINATION. *State v. Duffy.* Officer Mundy is on the stand, has been sworn, and has testified as to what her job is.

.1 She then testified that she had no present recollection of the robbery investigation. Lay the appropriate foundation to allow her to read from her police report dated June 1, Yr-0.

.2 Assume she can remember, but is a bit unclear on certain details, lay the appropriate foundation.

4.37 WITNESS EXAMINATION. Refer to 4.36.1. Having laid the foundation, the following testimony occurred:

By the prosecutor: Your honor, at this point I request the police report marked as State's Exhibit A For Identification be admitted into evidence as State's Exhibit A.

By Defense Counsel: Objection your honor, hearsay.

.1 State the correct ruling and reason.

Q (By the prosecutor): Did you speak to the tellers?

A: Yes.

Q: Who were they?

By Defense Counsel: Objection your honor, hearsay.

.2 State the correct ruling and reason.

Q: Did the robber say anything to Van Donk?

A: Yes.

Q: What did he say?

By Defense Counsel: Objection your honor, hearsay.

.3 State the correct ruling and reason.

A: Keep quiet and hand me the money.

Q: Did he have anything in his hand?

By Defense Counsel: Objection your honor, hearsay.

.4 State the correct ruling and reason.

A: Yes.

Q: What was it?

A: A big gun.

Q: Did Ms. Van Donk describe the robber?

A: Yes.

Q: How did she describe him?

By Defense Counsel: Objection your honor, hearsay.

.5 State the correct ruling and reason.

A: White, male 5'9", about 160 pounds.

Q: Were there any other customers in the bank at the time of the robbery?

By Defense Counsel: Objection your honor, hearsay.

Q: Did she recognize him?

A: Yes.

Q: Did she say how she recognized him?

A: Yes, he was a regular customer.

Q: Who was it?

By Defense Counsel: Objection your honor, hearsay.

.6 State the correct ruling and reason.

A: Arlo Duffy.

4.38 Defendant was charged with first-degree burglary of G.J.'s home. Trial is held nine months after the robbery occurred. G.J is on the stand. G.J. initially testifies that he did not get a good look at the burglar. After being shown statements that he made and signed during his police interview, he testified that, "I can't say for sure right now." G.J. agreed, however, that the witness statement shown to him was "an accurate reproduction of the questions that he was asked and the answers that he gave."

.1 Over defense objection, should the court permit the state to introduce G.J.'s signed statement to the police?

.2 Assume G.J.'s statement was tape recorded. Over defense objection, should the court permit the state to play the original audio recording of G.J.'s police interview?

4.39 Plaintiff moved across country and entrusted all his property to Harold Van Lines. Harold lost the property somewhere along the way. Plaintiff wants to introduce the notebook in which he listed all the items he owned as they were loaded on the truck. What options are available for using the notebook?

4.40 Plaintiff brings suit alleging a slip and fall on defendant's property. Defendant claims the fall never occurred and that the injuries claimed are from an occurrence before the alleged slip and fall. Defendant wants to introduce a memo summarizing an interview of plaintiff. The interview, conducted by an employee of the defendant's insurance company, occurred immediately after the fall. In the interview, plaintiff mentioned the prior injury, but did not mention any present injury. The insurance company employee has no present recollection, but as a matter of regular business practice, prepares this kind of memo in every case he handles. Is the memo admissible?

4.41 Refer to problem 4.39 Assume Harold Van Lines seeks to introduce the inventory of items placed on the truck to prove that the items claimed to be lost were never entrusted to it. The inventory was written in duplicate. Both the employee and the plaintiff initialed each page of the document as it was completed. Plaintiff kept one copy. Harold Van Lines kept the original. What options are available for using the document?

4.42 Plaintiff sues defendant to collect $100 due on the sale of merchandise. Defendant claims she only bought $10 worth and has paid that amount. Plaintiff's records are all computerized and show the value of the merchandise was $100. Can plaintiff introduce the computer records? What form would they take?

4.43 *Paula v. David and PDG.* Two police officers investigate the accident. Police officer Able interviewed Wanda. Police officer Baker interviewed Walter. Wanda tells Able the light was green for Paula. Walter tells Baker the light was green for David. Baker measures the skid marks and tells Able the measurements. Able puts all the above information in his report. When called to the stand by plaintiff, Able seeks to rely on his report and relate what Wanda, Walter and Baker said. Defendant objects based on hearsay. What ruling? Assume, Baker is on the stand, would that change the ruling?

4.44 *Paula v. David and PDG.* Paula has a sworn statement from the mechanic who repaired her car following the accident. Before trial, the mechanic died. To prove both the extent of her injuries as well as the extent of damage to her car, Paula seeks to introduce the sworn statement. Should such a statement be admissible?

4.45 Plaintiff was injured while operating a forklift manufactured by the defendant. Plaintiff claimed that the forklift was defectively designed because the operator cabin was not enclosed with a door and because defendant did not provide an adequate warning concerning the risks associated with the forklift. Plaintiff seeks compensatory and punitive damages.

Defendant seeks to introduce reports of independent engineers consulted by Defendant during the design of the forklift. Defendant has been unable to procure any employee of the independent engineering firm to testify. The reports contain the recommendation that the cab not be enclosed by doors. Plaintiff objects based on hearsay. What ruling?

4.46 Refer to problem 4.35.

.1 Adam wishes to introduce a portion of the nurses note, part of the hospital record, for the night in question that provides:

> 3:15 a.m. called Dr. B & informed him of bluish toes and cold and informed him about patient complaints of leg pain. Requested he come see patient. Dr. said call back in a.m. /s/ D. Loso, R.N.

Is this record admissible over an objection of hearsay?

.2 Bradman seeks to introduce a portion of the doctors' progress notes, part of the hospital record, for the day in question which provides:

> 7:30 a.m. Patient complaining of pain in the leg and numbness in toes. Toes are cold and bluish. Nurse should have insisted come in last night. Called to schedule surgery. /s/ Bradman, M.D.

Is this record admissible over an objection of hearsay?

.3 Nurse Loso, following Adam's complaint, and consistent with hospital policy, completed a document known as an incident report. This report, sent to the hospital's risk management committee, is designed to report objectively any life threatening incident so that the hospital can take steps to avoid having the incident, and potential harm repeated. Adam seeks to introduce this document as a business record. What result? Assume Dr. Bradman seeks to introduce the report. What result? Regardless of whether the report is admissible under the hearsay rule, should it be excluded for any other reason?

4.47   Plaintiff, the manufacturer of vodka, sues the defendant, a shipper of bulk liquid. Plaintiff alleges that defendant failed to clean adequately the large stainless steel trailer tank used to ship a large quantity of vodka. Specifically, defendant is alleged to have failed to clean the tanker truck after delivery a load of milk. On cross-examination of the defendant's president, the following took place.

Q: Isn't it true that the standard procedure of your company is to steam clean the tank after each use?

A: Yes.

Q: And isn't this especially important following a shipment of something that spoils, like milk?

A: Yes.

Q: And certainly it's true that when you use the tank for one purpose, like milk, and then use it for another purpose, like vodka, you must clean the tank?

A: Yes.

Q: In fact, didn't you say in your deposition that your standard procedure for such cleaning is for the truck depot to conduct the cleaning, and then, as a routine matter, send a report, really just a form with check marks and a signature, to the main office?

A: Yes.

Q: You haven't introduced any of those forms in this trial have you?

By Defense Counsel: Objection, your honor, hearsay.

What is the correct ruling?

4.48   *Donato v. Donato.*

.1 Witness Examination. At the hearing to determine custody, Gina would like to introduce the following documents. For Gina, attempt to introduce the documents in whatever manner is appropriate. For Paul, oppose the introduction of the evidence. The Reed Street address is the tavern beneath Paul's apartment.

```
┌─────────────────────────────────────────────────────────────────────┐
│  Police Department                          Case Yr-0-345             │
│  Complaint and Service Request Report                                 │
│                                                                       │
│  Nature of Complaint: ____drunk____    Location: 999 Reed St.____     │
│  Complainant: _____unknown___                    Address             │
│  Received by: sgt. James_____        Time:_____1:00 p.m.____     │
│                                                                       │
│  Details                                                              │
│                                                                       │
│  Phone call that there was fight at bar located this address. Officer │
│  arrived and saw two men arguing on street. Officer told both to move │
│  along and be quiet. No evidence of violence, and neither man         │
│  indicated needed help. No further action taken.                      │
│                                                                       │
│                                                          1/26/yr-0    │
│  _____     _____       _____      │
│   Approved By             Investigated By          Date               │
└─────────────────────────────────────────────────────────────────────┘
```

```
┌─────────────────────────────────────────────────────────────────────┐
│  Police Department                          Case Yr-1-5693            │
│  Complaint and Service Request Report                                 │
│                                                                       │
│  Nature of Complaint: _____Noise__     Location: _____999 Reed St.    │
│  Complainant: _____anonymous_                 Address             │
│  Received by: _____sgt. Spire      Time: _____1:15 p.m.          │
│                                                                       │
│  Details                                                              │
│                                                                       │
│  Complaint that noise from band was disturbing neighborhood. Went to  │
│  tavern at above address and spoke to Matthew Vitti. Band is noisy,   │
│  but did not appear excessive, given that location is Tavern and      │
│  apparently zoned for this activity.                                  │
│                                                                       │
│                                                          8/9/yr-1     │
│  _____     _____       _____      │
│   Approved By             Investigated By          Date               │
└─────────────────────────────────────────────────────────────────────┘
```

```
┌─────────────────────────────────────────────────────────────────────┐
│  Police Department                          Case Yr-1-3990            │
│  Complaint and Service Request Report                                 │
│                                                                       │
│  Nature of Complaint: ____drunk_       Location: _____999 Reed St.    │
│  Complainant: _____anonymous_                   Address             │
│  Received by: _____sgt. Spire      Time  11:05 p.m._             │
│                                                                       │
│  Details                                                              │
│                                                                       │
│  Drunk from tavern at above address was sleeping on sidewalk. Told to │
│  move. Became obnoxious, taken to station, released to wife. No other │
│  action taken.                                                        │
│                                                                       │
│                                                          6/3/yr-1     │
│  _____     _____       _____      │
│   Approved By             Investigated By          Date               │
└─────────────────────────────────────────────────────────────────────┘
```

.2 Paul seeks to introduce testimony of a private investigator who, if allowed will testify that he did a thorough search of records of the City

Department of Licenses and Inspections and found no record of any housing code violations for the apartment in which Paul lives.

4.49   Defendant is charged with possession of cocaine and tried in state court. State law provides that properly notarized "certificates of analysis" showing the results of lab analysis can be introduced as evidence that the substance seized from defendant was indeed cocaine. Defendant objects to the introduction of the cocaine and such a certificate purporting to show the substance is cocaine. What result?

4.50   *State v. Duffy.* Officer Gorham is unavailable for trial. Under Federal Rule of Evidence 803(8), may the prosecutor offer a certified copy of Officer Gorham's report? Could the report be introduced by the records clerk of the police station where Officer Gorham is assigned? Is there any other way in which the document could be used?

4.51   Defendant is charged with speeding, and driving while intoxicated, all while in a national park. At defendant's trial, the government called Officer Gillespie to testify and moved for the admission of a "certification notice" for the Intoxilyzer model 5000EN, serial number 68-010813. The notice indicates that the Intoxilyer was tested and found to be suitable for use in analyzing breath alcohol. This was the unit the officer used to administer a sobriety test on the defendant on the scene. Defendant objects. What result?

4.52   Refer to problem 4.34. The doctor that examined Alice dies before defendant goes on trial. As its first witness, the prosecutor calls the custodian of records at the clinic at which the doctor worked and seeks to introduce a report the doctor had prepared. The report contained graphic physical observations and findings of his examination of Alice. Defense counsel objects. What result?

4.53   Defendant, Simontov Yakobov, a.k.a. Yakov Yokubov, is charged with conspiracy to violate, and actual violation of, federal firearms statutes. It is alleged that he sold and shipped goods to Northern Ireland without an appropriate license.

> **.1** The prosecutor seeks to introduce certified copies of records of the Royal Ulster Constabulary to show that weapons containing specified serial numbers were found in Northern Ireland. Defendant objects. What ruling?

> **.2** To prove the defendant was not licensed by the federal government to export weapons, the prosecutor offers the signed, sworn, statement of the regional director of the Treasury Department's Bureau of Alcohol, Tobacco and Firearms (ATF). ATF is the appropriate licensing body. The statement provided:

Being duly sworn, I hereby certify that after a diligent search of the records in my control, I found no license issued to Simontov Yakobov which would authorize the sale and export of firearms.

Defendant objects. What ruling?

4.54 A Navy flight instructor was killed when her airplane, 3E955, crashed during a training flight. A Navy officer made the service's official investigation of the accident. This "JAG Report" made the following findings:

At approximately 1020, while turning crosswind without proper interval between other aircraft, 3E955 crashed, immediately caught fire and burned. At the time of the impact, the engine of 3E955 was operating, but at reduced power.

Due to the death of the pilot and the destruction of the plane, it is almost impossible to determine exactly what happened, but the most probable cause of the accident was the pilot's failure to maintain a proper interval between planes, causing the pilot to take an abrupt avoidance maneuver during which the plane stalled and then crashed.

Although the above sequence of events is the most likely to have occurred, it does not change the possibility that the crash was caused by a defect in the fuel control unit resulting in loss of power sufficient to conduct the avoidance maneuver.

At trial, plaintiff, the husband of the dead pilot, sought to introduce the JAG Report against defendant, the manufacturer of the airplane. Defendant's counsel objects based on hearsay. What ruling?

F. Additional Exceptions

4.55 Refer to problem 4.35. Adam seeks, in his case-in-chief, to introduce a textbook that during a deposition Bradman recognized as authoritative. The relevant portion states:

One of the clearest symptoms that a leg has been casted too tightly is the loss of feeling resulting from decreased circulation.

4.56 *Paula v. David and PDG.* Prior to trial, David was convicted of driving under the influence of alcohol, a misdemeanor, was sentenced to a weekend in jail, and had his license suspended.

.1 Paula seeks to have the record of conviction admitted into evidence in her lawsuit against David and PDG. Is the record admissible?

.2 Assume David's truck, after hitting Paula, ran up a sidewalk striking Harriet. Harriet died and David was tried and convicted of negligent homicide. David received an 18 month suspended sentence. Is this record of conviction admissible in the subsequent civil action?

.3 Does it matter that the evidence will also be used against PDG?

4.57 Plaintiff seeks to establish the value of her property by showing the value of comparable properties. To establish the value of comparable properties, plaintiff seeks to introduce the "Guide to Real Estate," a monthly publication produced by local real estate agencies, showing residential properties for sale in the metropolitan area. Defendant objects. What ruling?

4.58 Plaintiff brings suit on a life insurance policy, claiming he is entitled to double indemnity, because of the accidental death of the insured. The insurance company seeks to introduce a certified copy of the insured's death certificate. It is stated on the certificate that death was the result of a heart attack. Plaintiff objects. What ruling?

4.59 The United States brought an action seeking to obtain possession of a bell recovered from the C.S.S. Alabama, a Confederate commerce raider sunk by the Union Navy off the coast of Cherbourg, France in 1864. The United States claims the right to possession either by right of succession to all property of the former Confederate States of America or by right of capture. Defendant bought the bell in England and brought it back to the United States. When he put it up for auction, the United States Navy claimed that the bell was its property. How will the United States establish the historical facts of this case?

G. Preliminary Review

4.60   MOTION IN LIMINE. State v. Duffy. Trial is scheduled for next week. The judge has called a pretrial conference at which, among other things, she will entertain motions in limine. Prepare the arguments and oral motions you will make concerning the following evidence. Prepare to represent both the defendant and the state. **Be sure to fill out the questionnaire following your preparation.**

.1 Assuming Arlo does not admit the briefcase is his, on the issue of whether Arlo owns the brief case, the arresting police officer proposes to testify that Arlo said, when confronted with the case, "Hey, where did you find that?"

.2 On the issue of whether Arlo was the robber, the investigating police officer proposes to testify describing the clothes the robber was reportedly wearing at the time of the crime.

.3 Assume Arlo Duffy was convicted and another defendant, alleged to have helped Arlo rob the bank, is now on trial. A bank teller with firsthand knowledge wishes to testify that Arlo Duffy said, "Give me the money or you're dead."

.4 Assume the evidence is conflicting on the issue of whether the robber was armed at the time of the robbery. One teller testifies that while the robber was at the window of another teller, the other teller fell over from what later turned out to be a fatal heart attack. Just before she collapsed of the heart attack, the teller said, "Oh no! He's got a gun!"

.5 On the issue of how much money was taken from the bank, the prosecutor seeks to introduce the deposit and withdrawal slips for all customers of the bank on the day of the robbery.

H. Unavailability Required

4.61   Parker was driving his car at the intersection of Libbie and Grove, with his passenger Rachael, when there was a collision with Dan. The accident was witnessed by Walter. Parker sued Dan, calling Walter as a witness. Walter testified that Parker had the green light. The jury returned a verdict for Parker. Having seen that Parker was successful, Rachael brought suit against Dan. Between the judgment for Parker and the filing of Rachael's lawsuit, however, Walter died. In the subsequent lawsuit, may Rachael introduce that part of the transcript from the previous trial containing Walter's testimony?

4.62   Refer to problem 4.61 Assume instead that Parker and Rachael jointly bring suit against Dan. Walter is called to testify on behalf of plaintiffs, but the jury returns a verdict for Dan. Rachael then sues Parker. In the interim, Walter has been convicted of a felony and is serving time in a different state. In the second civil lawsuit, may Rachael introduce that part of the transcript from the previous trial containing Walter's testimony?

4.63   Refer to problem 4.61. Assume, however, that Dan calls Walter and he testifies that Dan had the green light. The jury, however, still returns a verdict against Dan. Rachael, the passenger, then brings suit against Dan. Dan again calls Walter to testify, but Walter refuses to testify. The court holds Walter in contempt. In the subsequent lawsuit, may Dan introduce that part of the transcript from the previous trial containing Walter's testimony?

4.64   Refer to problem 4.35. Bradman seeks to introduce the deposition of Harold Kellogg, a third nurse who was working the night in question. Harold testified as follows at a deposition:

> I was the charge nurse that evening and Diane Loso would have checked with me before she called Dr. Bradman. I just don't remember her saying anything about Bradman saying he wouldn't come in. I'm not even sure she asked him to come in.

Harold has subsequently moved out of state and resides across country, he is unavailable at trial. Is the deposition admissible?

4.65   Assume, for the purposes of this problem that the deposition referred to in the previous problem was introduced. Assume also that Adam's attorney recently sent an investigator to re-interview Harold at his new home. During that interview Harold was shown the medical records referred to in problem 4.46 and he said,

> I wasn't sure at the deposition, but that was before I'd had a chance to look at these medical records. Now it all comes back, again, I don't know what Bradman said to her, but I do remember Diane saying the toes felt cold. I'm not sure about the pain or the bluishness, but definitely the cold.

May the investigator testify as to Harold's statement?

4.66   Peter was injured when hole ripped open in the commercial airline in which he was flying on a trip to Hawaii. Peter brought suit against the airline alleging that a member of the ground crew failed to latch properly the cargo doors, causing the door to open during flight. Peter's deposition was taken by the airline.

> .1 Prior to trial, Peter died of his injuries. Would Peter's deposition be admissible even though the lawsuit now involves wrongful death?

> .2 Assume Peter's lawsuit is settled, Peter dies, and another passenger brings a lawsuit based on the same incident. Is Peter's deposition admissible by the plaintiff in the subsequent lawsuit?

> .3 Assume that in the subsequent lawsuit the plaintiff sues not only the airline, as Peter did, but has sued the manufacturer of the airplane on a products liability theory. Is Peter's deposition admissible?

4.67   Anthony is charged with fraud and racketeering.

> .1 At his preliminary hearing on the criminal charges, Anthony's lawyer, following a common practice among defense attorneys, chooses not to cross-examine the arresting police officer. After the preliminary hearing, but before trial, the police officer dies. May the prosecutor introduce the transcript of the officer's testimony from the preliminary hearing?

> .2 Bruno, an alleged coconspirator, testified at the grand jury. Bruno admitted his own guilt and implicated Anthony in the illegal activity as well. At trial, the prosecution calls Bruno expecting him to provide the same testimony. Bruno, however, invokes his Fifth Amendment privilege against self-incrimination and refuses to testify. The prosecutor now seeks to introduce a transcript of Bruno's grand jury testimony. Defense counsel objects. What ruling?

> .3 Assume that in the previous problem Bruno testified at the grand jury under a grant of immunity. At the grand jury, Bruno testified that neither he nor the defendant was involved in any scheme to defraud, nor were they engaged in racketeering. At trial, Anthony calls Bruno, hoping

that Bruno will provide the same exculpatory testimony. Bruno, however, invokes his Fifth Amendment privilege against self-incrimination and refuses to testify. Anthony now seeks to introduce a transcript of Bruno's grand jury testimony. The prosecutor objects. What ruling?

4.68 Colonel Wharton is on trial for manslaughter. The facts as alleged by the prosecutor are that Colonel Wharton deliberately drove his car head-on into an oncoming semi-tractor trailer truck resulting in his wife's death. The prosecutor seeks to introduce the testimony of a nurse who cared for Mrs. Wharton following the incident. If allowed, the nurse will testify that after being told by the doctor that she was dying from internal injuries caused by the accident, Mrs. Wharton indicated a need to talk to someone. When the nurse said she would listen, Mrs. Wharton said:

> Colonel Wharton put the accelerator on the floorboard and turned the car deliberately head-on into the tractor-trailer. He did it on purpose. He asked me if I wanted to go to eternity with him. This collision was not an accident. He said "we will go to eternity together."

.1 Is the nurse's testimony admissible? Would it make a difference if Mrs. Wharton did not die, but had slipped into a coma and Mr. Wharton was on trial for attempted murder?

.2 Assume Colonel Wharton was convicted of manslaughter. He then committed suicide. United Services Automobile Association (USAA), an insurer, brought a declaratory judgment action against the administrator of the estate of Colonel Wharton. USAA seeks a declaration of its obligations under a policy issued to Colonel Wharton covering his automobile. The policy specifically excludes coverage of intentional torts. Is Mrs. Wharton's statement admissible in this action?

.3 Assume that in addition to Mrs. Wharton, the driver of the tractor-trailer also died and Colonel Wharton is on trial for manslaughter in the death of the driver. Is the nurse's testimony admissible?

.4 Assume Mrs. Wharton lived and Colonel Wharton died. USAA refused to pay benefits under the insurance policy and Mrs. Wharton brings suit. May USAA introduce the testimony a passenger in the car who will testify that just before the collision Colonel Wharton said "we will go to eternity together?"

4.69 Paul brings an action to quiet title to a piece of real estate. Paul claims he has valid record title, having received it by intestate succession upon the death of his father, Grant. Grant was in actual possession of the property for five years, until his death one year ago. Paul has been in possession of the property since his father's death. Denny claims he is the rightful owner under a valid deed. Are the following statements admissible?

.1 Denny seeks to call a witness, Wayne, to testify that three years ago Wayne went to Grant and offered to buy the property. Wayne will testify that Grant said, "I'd love to sell it to you, but I'm only renting."

.2 Denny also seeks to call Walter who will testify that two years ago he was hunting on the property and Grant told him to get off. When Walter said he had the owner's permission, Grant said, "I don't care who you talked to, I rent this place and I want you off."

4.70 Andrea, a nurse, is charged with murder in the deaths of several patients at a hospital. After Andrea is arrested, Beverly, the head nurse who supervised Andrea is diagnosed as having cancer, and on her death bed says, "I can't go to my death with this on my conscience. I killed those patients, not Andrea." Before trial, Beverly dies. May Andrea introduce Beverly's statement? Suppose the statement had been, "Andrea and I felt so sorry for those patients, we just had to end their misery." Is the statement admissible by the prosecutor? Suppose the statement was, "I eased the way for the first three patients by myself; Andrea was on her own for the last four." Is it admissible?

4.71 Defendant is charged with racketeering and murder. The government alleges that defendant operated a criminal organization that rigged gasoline pumps to over-charge customers. It also alleges that defendant killed one of the owners of the rigged gas stations, Victor, when it became known that Victor was going to cooperate with the police.

The government seeks to introduce the testimony of Gail, Victor's girlfriend, who will testify that Victor told her that the defendant had warned him to "be careful what you say. If I find out you are talking to the cops, it won't be so good for you." Defendant makes a hearsay objection. How should the court rule?

I. Additional Constitutional Concerns

4.72 Defendant is charged with receiving stolen property. To prove the car was stolen, the prosecutor seeks to introduce the felony conviction of the person who allegedly transferred the car to the defendant. The conviction is for stealing the car in question. Defense counsel objects. What ruling? Suppose that as a matter of substantive criminal law the prosecutor must show the conviction of the thief in order to obtain a conviction of the receiver. Would this affect your answer?

4.73 In problem 4.34 the prosecutor wishes to introduce the testimony of a psychiatric social worker who has been counseling Alice since the rape. If permitted, the social worker will testify that three months after the incident, Alice told her that Doug had on several occasions tried to pull down her jeans, and touch her places her mommy told her not to let people touch. When she fought and screamed, she said the Doug would hit her. Defense counsel objects based on hearsay and the Sixth Amendment Confrontation Clause. What ruling? Would it make a difference if Alice herself will not testify? Would it matter if the testimony referred to in problem 4.34 had or had not been admitted?

4.74 Dustin and his girlfriend, Angela, are charged with murdering three people. During the trial, while in jail, Angela became acquainted with Robert, another prisoner. As a ruse, Robert told Angela she could escape responsibility for the murders if he (Robert) who was already serving a life sentence falsely claimed responsibility for the murder. Robert told Angela that in order to make the confession believable, he would need to be able to furnish proof of his involvement by leading authorities to the victims' bodies. Angela prepared and provided Robert with maps and notes describing the locations where the bodies were buried. Robert turned the maps and notes over to law enforcement. Using the maps, police officers discovered the bodies. The prosecutor seeks to introduce the maps and notes against both Dustin and Angela who object asserting the maps are hearsay and violate the Confrontation Clause. Neither Dustin nor Angela will testify at trial, asserting their Fifth Amendment rights. What result?

4.75 Refer to problem 4.35. Assume, however, the suit is against the hospital. Also, assume Adam never called his mother during the night. At approximately 4:00 a.m. the morning in question, Nurse Loso was in the room adjacent to Adam's. She testified that she heard a loud thump against the wall in Adam's room and immediately left to investigate. She discovered Adam on the floor and asked him what had happened. Based on what Adam told her and her personal observations, she made the following notation on Adam's clinical record:

> Found pt [patient] on floor — Apparently crawled out end of bed — trying to get to BR [bathroom] — had called for help but not a quick enough response.

Approximately eleven hours after Adam's fall, his parents arrived at the hospital unaware of the previous night's events. After learning from the station nurse that Adam had fallen, the Klares went to their son in his hospital room and asked him what had happened. Over the hospital's objection, Mrs. Klare testified as follows:

Q: Then what happened?

A: We ran into the room and we said, "Adam, what in the world's happened?" And he said, "Oh, Mother, it was terrible."

Q: What else did he say?

A: He said, "I put the call bell on, or the call light." He said, "I put the call bell on and I waited and I waited and no one came. I waited again and put the call bell on again two or three times." He'd keep punching it he said. "And no one came to help me. And I called out, 'help! Help me!' and no one came."

Q: Did he tell you how he managed to actually get someone to come?

A: He showed me that he got out through the rails, the split rails. He was smaller than he is now. He told me, he said, "I got out through these rails, Mother. And I fell. I hit my head and I hit my leg." And he said, "The nurse came in finally when I fell and she was about mad at me. She bawled me out."

Klare's attorney then showed her Nurse Loso's notations on the clinical record, and asked her, through a series of questions, if the notations confirmed what Adam told her that next morning. Mrs. Klare testified that the two were consistent. There was additional testimony directly on the question of whether the hospital's response was tardy. Mrs. Klare testified that a couple of days after the incident in question:

> Nurse Loso came up in the hall, my husband and I were standing in the hall, and by Adam's room, and she said — she was crying and she said, "Mr. and Mrs. Klare, I am so sorry. I just couldn't get to Adam. I was with another patient. We're so short-handed and I was with another patient and I couldn't get to Adam. The call light was on and I heard him call, but I couldn't get to him." Nurse Loso, on direct examination, admitted apologizing to the Klares but denied ever telling them that the hospital was short-staffed or that she had heard the call bell. On cross-examination, Klare's attorney brought out that in a deposition taken a year earlier, Nurse Kennedy stated that she did not remember exactly what she had told the Klares.

Was the court correct in permitting Mrs. Klare's testimony?

4.76   Refer to 4.1.20. Assume the party seeks to introduce the envelopes in which the bids arrived, upon which there are postmarks. Are the envelopes admissible?

4.77   Defendant is on trial for conspiracy to commit murder. To establish the conspiracy and the timeframe within which the conspiracy took place, the prosecutor seeks to introduce a letter and the postmarked envelope in which it was sent. The letter contains statements from which the jury could infer that the sender was soliciting defendant to kill someone. Neither the defendant nor the coconspirator will testify at trial. Defense counsel objects. What ruling?

4.78   Refer to problem 4.9. Arlo objects to the introduction of any of the testimony under 801(d)(1)(c) claiming a violation of his Sixth Amendment Confrontation Clause rights. What result?

Chapter 5

LAY AND EXPERT OPINIONS

A. Lay Opinion

5.1 Is any of the following testimony permissible lay opinion?

.1 *Paula v. David and PDG.* Walter seeks to testify that he was standing beside the road when,

> **A.** "I heard this car zoom behind me on the cross street. It had to be going at least 60."
>
> **B.** "I heard Paula's car speeding down the road."
>
> **C.** "I saw Paula's car speeding down the road."
>
> **D.** "I saw Paula's car coming about 60 miles per hour down the road."

.2 *Donato v. Donato.* Mrs. Donato will testify that, "Paul's apartment is a pig sty. He never cleans it up, and it's got roaches."

.3 *Donato v. Donato.* Mrs. Donato will testify that, "Paul's apartment is simply too rundown for children. And worse, the neighborhood is simply dangerous."

.4 A customs inspector wishes to testify that he suspected the defendant was illegally importing food because the inspector could smell "oranges."

.5 *State v. Duffy.* Arlo raises as a defense that he was taking medication at the time of the robbery and that this medication made him psychotic, thus reducing his criminal liability. Sherry Van Donk will testify that "Arlo looked calm and collected. He certainly didn't look insane or crazy or anything like that."

.6 *State v. Duffy.* Glenda Berg seeks to testify that when approached by the robber, Sherry Van Donk, "looked like she was very scared."

.7 *Paula v. David and PDG.* Wanda seeks to testify that at the time of the accident David looked drunk. Assume the judge allows the testimony, what type of questions would you ask on cross-examination?

.8 *State v. Duffy.* Sherry Van Donk will testify that the photograph of the robber taken from the surveillance camera in the bank looks like the defendant, Arlo Duffy.

.9 *State v. Duffy.* Glover, Arlo's probation officer will testify that he has met with Arlo four times in a two-month period, for a total of more than seventy minutes. He then seeks to identify Arlo as the person in the photograph of the robber taken from the surveillance camera in the bank.

.10 On the issue of why her husband was depressed, a wife seeks to testify that it was because he failed to receive a promotion at work and that this was part of a pattern of what she felt he believed were recent personal failures on his part.

.11 Defendant is on trial for fraudulent sale "green cards" to illegal immigrants. At trial, Sien, a former government employee and coconspirator, testified about defendant's role in the green card scheme, including defendant's acquisition of fourteen clients, and a total of $70,000 paid to Sien in exchange for the green cards. The jurors are presented with audio and video recordings of all of the conversations between defendant and Sien. Near the end of his testimony, the government asks:

> Q: Mr. Sien, at all times that you were dealing with defendant, was he aware that paying money in exchange for the green cards was illegal?

> A: I think we must be kidding here. This gentleman knew all the time that everything he was doing was illegal. One does not buy a green card on the street for money. Come on, let's stop pretending here. We are not stupid people, are we?

.12 Plaintiff alleges that, while she was driving her car, she was struck head-on by defendant who was driving a truck. On direct examination, defendant testifies that he was lawfully driving when an eight-year-old darted between parked cars, causing him to swerve to avoid hitting the child. As a result, he did strike plaintiff's car. He is then asked,

> Q: If you had not swerved, would you have hit the child?

> A: Yes.

> Q: You have heard testimony concerning the plaintiff's injuries?

> A: Yes.

> Q: If you had not swerved to avoid hitting the child, would you have caused more damage to the child than was suffered by plaintiff?

> A: The child would have died.

.13 Refer to problem 1.6. Plaintiff calls four co-workers who will testify to their personal knowledge of the similar incidents and that in their opinion plaintiff's discharge was racially motivated.

5.2 WITNESS INTERVIEW. *Donato v. Donato.* You represent Gina.

You would like to have testimony concerning Gina's ability as a mother. You think Gina's own mother/father might make a good witness. Interview Gina's mother/father to determine whether she/he can and should testify as to Gina's fitness as a parent. **Your instructor will provide the person playing the father/mother with confidential information. Be sure to fill out the joint questionnaire following the simulation.**

5.3 WITNESS EXAMINATION. Using the information obtained in 5.2 conduct the direct examination of Gina's mother/father. Your instructor will provide you with additional information if you did not do 5.2.

B. Expert Opinion

5.4 Defendant is on trial for providing marijuana to her minor daughter. The prosecutor calls Brandi who, if allowed, will testify that she and the defendant have a lengthy history of smoking marijuana together. She will testify that she saw defendant provide defendant's daughter with a lit marijuana water pipe and allowed the daughter to inhale from the water pipe. According to Brandi, defendant prepared the water pipe for use, before giving it to her daughter, by scraping matter from the inside of the water pipe. She recognized the substance that the defendant scraped from the inside of the water pipe as marijuana residue that that contained "chunks" of marijuana. Defense counsel objects. What ruling?

5.5 Defendant is charged with possession of cocaine with intent to distribute. Over defense counsel's objections, the government introduced the testimony of several police officers who had defendant under surveillance for a number of days. In that testimony the police officers testified that

- defendant engaged in "suspicious" movements;
- defendant was engaging in counter-surveillance driving;
- certain terms used by Defendant and informant were code words for a drug deal, a common practice of narcotics dealers;
- defendant's use of a rental car was consistent with the practices of an experienced drug trafficker;
- the manner of hiding the cocaine was consistent with the practices of experienced drug traffickers; and
- the large quantity and high purity of the cocaine indicated that Defendant was close to the source of the cocaine.

On appeal, the Government admits that no foundation was provided establishing the testimony as expert opinion. The Government contends, however, that the testimony was permissible lay opinion. How should the appellate court rule?

5.6 Which of the following are proper subjects for expert testimony? In any of the cases, should expert testimony be required?

.1 In a medical malpractice action, plaintiff proposes to have a physician testify that it is improper medical procedure to leave a surgical sponge in a patient following an operation.

.2 *State v. Duffy.* Assume Sherry Van Donk can make a positive identification. In defense, Arlo calls a psychologist to the stand to testify concerning the inherent weakness of eyewitness identification, especially when a weapon is involved.

.3 In a personal injury action, plaintiff, an 18-year-old quadriplegic, seeks to introduce the testimony of an economist concerning his potential earnings had he not been injured.

.4 In an action to quiet title, plaintiff seeks to have a law professor testify that, according to the law of the jurisdiction, a properly conducted title search would have placed defendant on inquiry notice that plaintiff had superior title at the time defendant acquired his deed.

.5 In an action for attorney's fees following a successful civil rights lawsuit, counsel seeks to call an attorney who will testify that she has read the entire record in the case and in her opinion the fee requested is a reasonable attorney's fee.

.6 Refer to problem 5.1.8. Assume the photograph is unclear. The prosecutor calls an expert to make a comparison of the bone structure of the defendant with the bone structure of the person in the photograph. If allowed, the expert will then identify the defendant as the person in the photograph.

.7 Plaintiff, in a personal injury action arising out of an airplane crash, seeks to call a psychologist who has studied the survivors of airplane disasters and who will testify to the psychological stress the passengers experience when it becomes apparent that the plane will crash.

.8 In a criminal prosecution for assault and attempted rape of a six-year-old, the defendant testifies in his own behalf. In rebuttal the prosecutor seeks to have a psychologist testify that the defendant is a compulsive liar.

.9 In the previous problem, suppose the prosecutor seeks to have the psychologist testify that the victim, who has already testified, knows the difference between telling the truth and lying.

5.7 In an action for violation of state obscenity laws, the legal standard requires applying contemporary community standards. Defendant seeks to introduce the testimony of a professional pollster who conducted a survey among fourteen hundred households in the city in which the trial is taking place. Seventy-five percent of all respondents did not find the material obscene. The prosecutor objects. What ruling?

5.8 In an action based on diversity of citizenship, Mr. Perry, a New York resident, brings a medical malpractice action arising out of treatment begun in an emergency room in Tennessee. Perry alleges that Dr. Duke mistreated a chainsaw cut to his knee by failing to read a lab report within 24 hours of the injury and by thereafter providing improper antibiotic treatment. Both actions, he claims, caused him to develop degenerative arthritis in his knee. State law provides:

> In a medical malpractice action, a person is incompetent to testify as to matters the plaintiff must prove unless the person he was licensed to practice in the state or a contiguous bordering state a profession or specialty which would make the expert testimony relevant to the issues in the case and has practiced this profession or specialty in one of these states during the year preceding the date that the alleged injury or wrongful act.

.1 Perry calls to the stand an emergency room staff nurse who will testify that

A. Hospital policy requires lab reports of this kind be completed and returned to the patient's record within 24 hours.

B. The particular lab report in question was returned within 24 hours.

C. The doctor did not meet the accepted standard of care when he failed to read the report in a timely manner.

.2 Perry calls to the stand Dr. Jones who testifies as follows:

Q: Would you tell us your name?

A: Dr. Rhonda Jones.

Q: Where do you live?

A: New York City

Q: Are you employed?

A: Yes, I am on the faculty of the Albany Medical Center.

Q: Are you licensed?

A: Yes, I am licensed in two states; both New York and Massachusetts.

By Defense Counsel: Objection, your honor.

What are the likely grounds for the objection and how should the court rule?

.3 Duke takes the witness stand to testify that the cause of plaintiff's continuing injury is not a failure to read a lab report. Rather, the cause of Perry's degenerative arthritis was the chainsaw cutting into his knee.

5.9   Which of the following involve a proper expert testifying about a proper subject matter?

.1 In problem 4.54 involving the crash of the Navy airplane, plaintiff, the spouse of the victim, seeks to testify. Plaintiff, himself is a navy pilot, but has never flown the type of plane involved in the crash. Having reviewed the investigation information, he will testify that in his opinion the crash was caused by a defective fuel mechanism resulting in a loss of power.

.2 In a criminal prosecution for sale of cocaine, the prosecutor offers the testimony of an FBI agent. The FBI agent has received training in drug identification based on appearance. He has been confirmed in his identifications on many occasions and seeks to testify that the drug sold was cocaine.

.3 Landlord, the owner of 500 apartment units, sued a tenant for breach of the lease agreement, contending that the tenant had committed $3,000 worth of damage to the apartment. The landlord seeks to testify as to the cost of the damage to the property.

.4 Plaintiff, a cattle rancher, sues the defendant, a feed supplier, for negligence in preparing feed for plaintiff's cattle. Plaintiff calls as a witness his neighbor, also a farmer. The neighbor will testify that he has been a cattle rancher for 40 years. He started working soon after he dropped out of high school, and, except for a short time while in the military, has worked on cattle ranches ever since. He will state that, based on his examination of plaintiff's cattle, the cause of their illness is contaminated feed.

.5 Plaintiff, 16 years old, was paralyzed when he dived into defendant's pool. Defendant is a private club. In an action against the club, defendant seeks to introduce the testimony of an experienced swim instructor and high school teacher who will testify to the effect that teenagers have a propensity to be reckless around a swimming pool, and not pay attention when diving into the pool.

5.10 State v. Duffy. To support his alibi defense, Arlo introduced a photograph of himself and his mother that he says was taken on the day of the bank robbery. To establish the falsity of Arlo's alibi, the prosecutor, over objection, introduced the testimony of an astronomer who said that the photograph offered by Arlo could not have been taken on the day of the robbery. On appeal, Arlo challenges the admissibility of the astronomer's testimony. The following quotation is taken from the trial court's written opinion:

> Defendant's motion involves the admission of a novel application of mathematical and astronomical theories of Dr. Ciupik. Ciupik testified that he was an associate astronomer at the Adler Planetarium in Chicago, working chiefly as the Observatory Director; he had authored two children's books on astronomy, worked as a consultant for Rand, McNally, and written articles for McGraw-Hill's Yearbook of Science and Technology. He had taught astronomy to gifted high school students, and was a member of a local professional organization. He was accepted by the court, without objection, as an expert capable of making astronomical calculations. Ciupik testified that as it revolves around the sun, the earth is fixed in its orientation towards the North Star. The sun's path as we perceive it in the daytime sky therefore repeats itself from

year to year. Twice a year, on dates equidistant from the summer or winter solstices, the sun will be in precisely the same location with respect to both the horizon and the North Star. Ciupik then expounded the theory that if one knew the compass orientation of an object in a photograph, it would be possible to date that photograph by: 1) measuring the directional angle of the shadow cast by that object to determine the azimuth of the sun (the azimuth of the sun is its angle from true south); and 2) measuring the angle of elevation of a complete shadow cast by another object in the photograph to determine the altitude of the sun (the altitude of the sun is the angle formed by its elevation about the horizon). Ciupik stated that the intersection point of the altitude and the azimuth, defining the sun's position in the sky, corresponds to the only two dates of the year on which the photo could have been taken.

Ciupik further testified that he could determine those two dates by entering his finding for altitude and azimuth on a "sun chart." Although Ciupik could not ascertain who prepared the chart, or even under whose supervision it had been prepared some fifteen years ago, he testified that he had verified its accuracy with an Analog Computer and through continued usage. He stated, however, that the lines on the chart corresponding to the sun's path in the daytime sky were based on the sun's path on the 22nd day of each month, and that one would be compelled to interpolate the data obtained through his reverse calculations in order to determine the sun's position on any other day. Moreover, the only purpose for which the chart had been used in the past was to measure the height of lunar mountains. The chart, a pivotal piece of evidence, was admitted over objection that it was unverified hearsay, and therefore formed an inadequate basis for Ciupik's calculations. On cross-examination, Ciupik admitted that although he had made numerous measurements of lunar mountains with the aid of the chart, neither he nor anyone else as far as he knew had ever used it prior to this trial for the purpose of dating a photograph. Nor could he point to any published text suggesting or detailing the method one would use for such calculations.

How should the court rule? What might the prosecutor or astronomer have done to increase the likelihood that the trial court's decision would be upheld?

5.11   *Donato v. Donato.* Paul claims Gina abuses the children. Paul, therefore, seeks to introduce expert testimony about the general characteristics of the battered child syndrome (BCS). BCS has previously been described by this expert as follows:

BCS indicates that a child of tender years found with a certain type of injury has not suffered those injuries by accidental means, but rather is the victim of child abuse. The diagnosis is used in connection with very young children, usually four years of age or younger, who cannot testify themselves. It is based upon a finding that such child exhibits evidence of, among other things, subdural hematoma, fractures in various stages of healing, soft tissue swelling or skin bruising. Also pertinent to the diagnosis is evidence that the child is generally undernourished and that the severity of injuries on his body is inconsistent with the parents' story of their occurrence.

In addition, the expert seeks to testify that Ellen exhibits symptoms consistent with the syndrome, and he therefore believes that she has been abused. In deciding whether this testimony should be admitted, what factors should the court take into consideration? Would it make a difference if the expert was to testify that the defendant had characteristics of a child abuser?

5.12 In a lawsuit involving the question of whether a child with a mental disability was receiving a federally mandated appropriate education, the parents seek to call a special education expert to testify. Reproduced below is the expert's resume. How might you use this resume to qualify the person as an expert?

RESUME

Samantha Tucker
90 Elm Street
Calhoun, Columbia

Education

Ph.D.	University of Michigan, Ann Arbor, Michigan Educational Psychology/Special Education, Yr-5.
M.Ed.	University of California at Los Angeles. Special Education, Yr-10.
B.A.	University of Richmond, Richmond, Virginia Psychology, Yr-17.

Employment

Yr-5 to present.	Assistant Superintendent, Special Education, York, New Hampshire.
Yr-10 - Yr-7.	Director, Steele School, a private residential school for children with severe emotional disabilities. Dover, Mass.
Yr-14 - Yr-12	Principal, Harris Special Education Center, public school for children with wide range of physical and mental disabilities. Harris, N.Y.
Yr-12 - Yr-17	Teacher, Special Education, Harris Special Education Center, Harris, N.Y.

Other Professional Experience

Adjunct Faculty, York Community College.
Consultant, York Association for Retarded Citizens.
Consultant/Expert Witness Special Education Litigation.

Professional Affiliations

Council for Exceptional Children (Board of Directors Yr-5 to present); American Association on Mental Deficiency; National Association for Retarded Citizens.

Publications

"Special Education Centers and Their Conflict with Mainstreaming"; "Educational Programming and the Severely Retarded"; "Parents, Schools and Conflicts Over Education."

5.13 Refer to problem 5.8. Assume the plaintiff calls Dr. Edmonds. After being qualified, he testifies as follows:

Q: Dr. Edmonds, are you familiar with Mr. Perry?

A: Well, I've never met the gentleman, but I have reviewed his medical records.

Q: Which medical records?

A: I reviewed all the records of the emergency room where Mr. Perry went on the day of his injury. Then I obtained copies of his medical records from his present treating physician, Dr. Williams.

Q: Do you have information concerning Mr. Perry from any other source?

A: Yes. I had quite a long conversation with Dr. Williams concerning his treatment of Mr. Perry.

Q: Did these records indicate whether Mr. Perry was suffering from any permanent damage to his knee?

Defense Counsel: I object, your honor, this is hearsay.

Court: Overruled.

A: Yes, there was a reduction of mobility in the knee.

Q: Now, you indicated that you spoke to Dr. Williams. Specifically, what did he tell you?

Defense Counsel: Objection, your honor, hearsay.

Court: Objection sustained.

Q: Based on your review of these records, do you have an opinion as to the cause of the damage to the knee?

A: Yes.

Q: Is that opinion consistent with Dr. Williams' opinion?

Defense Counsel: Objection, your honor, hearsay.

Court: Objection sustained.

Were the court's rulings correct?

5.14 *Paula v. David and PDG.* Paula calls to the stand, Harold Hughes, Ph.D., an "accident reconstruction expert."

.1 After testifying to his qualifications, the court qualifies him as an expert. Paula then asks:

Q: Do you have an opinion as to the cause of the accident?

Defense Counsel: I object your honor. There is no basis for this witness to give an expert opinion.

How should the judge rule?

.2 Assume the judge overrules the objection and the witness proceeds to give his opinion and nothing more. On cross-examination, the following occurs:

Q: Dr. Hughes, isn't it true that you base your testimony on a limited number of different types of information?

A: I'm not sure I would agree.

Q: In fact, the information supporting your conclusion is based entirely on what other people have told you?

A: Not entirely. As I've testified, I have years of experience in this area.

Q: But you did not see this accident yourself?

A: No I didn't.

Q: In fact, would it be fair to say that you received most of your information from questioning bystanders and the plaintiff?

A: Yes, that would be a fair statement.

At this point, what should defense counsel do? If defense counsel was prepared to conduct this line of questioning on cross-examination, was there anything she could have done on direct examination?

5.15 Refer to problem 5.8. Having qualified Dr. Williams, Mr. Perry's treating physician as an expert, prepare the shortest possible direct examination in which he will testify to the causal connection between the failure to read the lab report and Mr. Perry's permanent leg disability.

5.16 In the previous problem,

.1 Would Dr. Williams be able to testify, "In my opinion, Dr. Duke committed malpractice"?

.2 Would Dr. Williams be able to testify that, "In my opinion, Dr. Duke's treatment of Mr. Perry fell below the standard of acceptable medical practice within this state"?

.3 Would Dr. Williams be able to testify, "In my opinion acceptable medical practice would be to have read the lab report within 24 hours, and then administer intravenous antibiotics. This would have stopped the infection and there would have been no loss of mobility in the leg"?

5.17 In a criminal prosecution for first degree murder, defendant calls the stand a psychiatrist who, if allowed, will testify, "In my opinion, the defendant's addiction to the drugs that were prescribed for him put him in such a cycle of depression that he was unable to take any premeditated action." Is this testimony objectionable?

5.18 WITNESS EXAMINATION. *Donato v. Donato.* Paul offers as a witness the Reverend Anthony Lonagoni, Jesuit Priest at St. Rita's, the church the Donato's attend. A summary of the Father's deposition follows:

I am a 62 year old Jesuit Priest, presently in St. Rita's Parish, here in town. I grew up in Milan, Italy, attending a Jesuit Seminary and eventually studying at the Gregorian Institute in Rome. In Yr-18 I published an article entitled "Relating the Catholic Church to the Real World of God" in the Catholic Journal.

In Yr-17 I was transferred to the United States, where I moved from parish to parish until transferred to St. Rita's in Yr-10. In addition to directing church, my primary responsibilities since being in the United States have been teaching. I presently teach in the primary and secondary schools run by St. Rita's. I teach Latin and several religion courses. Since being in the United States I have taken 2 courses in psychology and one course in counseling. I confirmed Ellen and Richard and baptized Allen.

I am a firm follower of the Catholic Church's position concerning sex outside of marriage. It is contrary to the teachings of the Scriptures and the 1975 Vatican Declaration on Sexual Ethics. My years of experience indicate such activity drives people away from the Church and a life with God. I have noticed this with Allen and Ellen. Since Gina divorced Paul, the children have attended mass and communion less frequently.

I was consulted by Paul Donato concerning the children several months ago. I urged him to seek custody of his children. Placement of the children with Paul would enhance their moral and religious interests in addition to their general welfare.

I have visited Paul's apartment on several occasions. It is a small, but clean, two bedroom apartment located over a tavern. I am somewhat concerned that it is located over the tavern since it can be noisy at night, but it is a safe and friendly neighborhood.

For Paul, conduct an examination of Father Lonagoni, qualifying him as an expert and eliciting appropriate testimony. For Gina, oppose the testimony of Father Lonagoni.

Chapter 6

AUTHENTICATION

6.1 In a breach of contract action, plaintiff claims that a written contract was executed. Which if any of the following is a permissible way to authenticate the document plaintiff claims is the contract?

.1 Plaintiff seeks to introduce the document by testifying that he saw defendant sign this document and that this is the contract.

.2 Plaintiff seeks to introduce the document by testifying that he has dealt with defendant for six years, that they have corresponded regularly during that period, and that they have entered into six written contracts. Each of the contracts, including the one in this litigation, was negotiated by phone with documents exchanged by mail. Further, plaintiff will testify that, although he has never personally met the defendant prior to bringing this lawsuit, he recognizes the signature on the document in question as that of the defendant.

.3 Plaintiff will testify that he has never had contact with the defendant before the present contract. He knows that the signature is defendant's, however, because he has compared the signature on the contract with defendant's signature on the deposition taken in this action.

.4 Assume the defendant claims that he never signed the contract and that the document plaintiff is seeking to introduce contains his forged signature. What standard should the judge use to determine the admissibility of the document?

6.2 WITNESS EXAMINATION. *State v. Duffy.* Assume Arlo signed the statement he made after his arrest. The statement, however, was not notarized. Officer Gorham is unavailable at trial. Authenticate Arlo's statement, questioning any witnesses of your choice.

6.3 Sylvia is on trial for the murder of Harold. The prosecutor alleges Sylvia and Harold had an affair and Harold broke off the relationship. Despondent, Sylvia murdered Harold and attempted suicide. The prosecutor seeks to call Maude, Harold's widow. If allowed, Maude will testify that while doing the laundry she found a note from Sylvia to Harold, signed by Sylvia. The note said, "I love you Harold. Why won't you dump Maude?" The letter itself was destroyed when Maude, in a rage over finding it, tore it up and tossed it out the window. Sylvia's attorney objects to Maude's testimony based on lack of authentication of the letter. Must the letter be authenticated, and if so what possible ways are there to do it?

6.4 WITNESS EXAMINATION. *Donato v. Donato.* You represent

Paul Donato. Paul has an answering machine. After filing the custody suit, Paul came home and the following, and nothing else, was recorded on the machine:

> "Why don't you give up, you're going to lose the kids one way or the other."

The recording has been erased. Paul is convinced the caller was Gina. Prepare the direct examination of Paul to introduce this statement into evidence.

6.5   Assume that in the previous problem, Paul is convinced that the caller was Sam. Which if any of the following is a permissible means to authenticate the recorded message?

> **.1** Paul will testify that he has known Sam for several years. They coached together for many years in the basketball program at the local Catholic Church. He estimates they have talked on the phone at least 100 times, and well over that number of times in person.

> **.2** Paul will testify that he has never met Sam personally, but that on at least six occasions when he called Gina's house to talk about visitation with the kids, a male voice sounding just like the voice on the answering machine answered, saying, "Sam here."

> **.3** Paul will testify that he has never had contact with the defendant Sam before the present action. He knows that the voice was Sam's, however, because he has heard Sam talking to Gina in the courthouse hallway and recognized the voice as the same one on the answering machine.

6.6   An action was brought to denaturalize the defendant for failure to disclose membership in a Ukrainian Nazi police organization during World War II. In order to prove membership in the organization, the government seeks to introduce two documents that it purports are 1) an application for insurance filled out at the time the defendant joined the organization, and 2) a form used when membership in the organization was ended. The documents were obtained from the Ukrainian government and were certified by a Ukrainian official authorized to release the documents to foreign governments. Both documents contained the defendant's name. The government called two witnesses. The first, an expert on the holocaust testified that he had seen documents such as these before, and that these were very similar in appearance. A second witness, an expert on written documents, testified that in his opinion, the documents had been executed no later than the dates contained on the documents. Should the trial court allow the introduction of the documents? Why or why not?

6.7   In which, if any, of the following questions has the evidence been properly authenticated? What additional information you would like to have before admitting the item into evidence?

.1 In an action for failure to pay income tax, the government seeks to introduce a certified computer printout of its records showing that it has no record of defendant ever filing an income tax return.

.2 In order to show that fire destroyed a courthouse in the city of Columbia 60 years ago, the proponent seeks to introduce a newspaper dated 60 years ago, with "The Columbia Times-Dispatch" printed on its masthead. The newspaper contains an article that says the police chief reported the destruction of the courthouse. Regardless whether it is authentic, should the newspaper be excluded because it is hearsay?

.3 *Donato v. Donato.* Mrs. Donato seeks to introduce certified copies of reports from the city Department of Licensing and Inspections. The reports were the result of an inspection occasioned by the structural damage caused in the storm.

.4 Criminal prosecution is brought against a corporation for allegedly paying illegal bribes to an official of a foreign government. As part of its defense, the corporation seeks to introduce photocopies of relevant foreign statutes that it claims indicate the payments were fees, not bribes.

6.8 Refer to problem 4.41. Having laid the foundation for the business records exception, what else must be done to authenticate the document?

6.9 To prove that a person was admitted to Albany Law School, plaintiff seeks to introduce the acceptance letter received by the person. How would plaintiff authenticate the letter?

6.10 In which, if any, of the following questions has the evidence been properly authenticated? What additional information you would like to have before admitting the item into evidence?

.1 An undercover police officer received a call that he would like to testify was from the defendant. He did not recognize the voice. The substance of the conversation was an arrangement to purchase drugs. Pursuant to the telephone conversation, the police officer went to an address looking for someone wearing a trench coat. At that address, the defendant approached him and sold him drugs.

.2 In a criminal prosecution, defendant is alleged to have murdered his girl friend and then to have attempted suicide. The prosecutor seeks to introduce a series of four typewritten notes found lying near the victim and defendant. The first note refers to personal problems the defendant is having, says the victim is the cause of these problems, that she would pay, and that the end was near for them both. The note then made provision for the distribution of the defendant's estate. The second note says that a third party "Arthur," was the cause of the defendant's problems. The third note was a love letter purportedly from Arthur to the victim. The fourth note, found in defendant's clothing asks the finder to notify defendant's family of his death.

.3 In a criminal prosecution for homicide, the defendant is charged with killing his wife and two children. As part of the prosecutor's attempt to prove motive, he seeks to establish that the defendant was unfaithful to his wife. As part of that effort, the prosecutor calls a former girl friend of the defendant's. The girlfriend will testify that she received a present of a black and red (their high school colors) negligee from the defendant the day before he married his wife. The day before the wedding, defendant, the witness will testify, came to her office, said he was getting married the next day and that he had a gift for her. When she went out to the car she found the negligee.

6.11 A husband and wife are on trial for selling heroin. The government alleges that the defendants sold the drugs to a police informant. There is testimony that the informant met the defendants in the back of a van where the sale took place. The informant left the van, got into his car and then drove to the police station and turned the drugs over to the police. Having received a signal from the informant upon leaving the van, the police followed the van and arrested the husband and wife when they returned to their home. While the van was under surveillance during the sale, the police did not actually see the sale. The informant died between the day of arrest and trial. Defendants oppose the admission of the heroin. What result?

6.12 DRAFTING. As a part-time prosecutor for a small rural county, draft procedures the police department should follow upon seizing suspected drugs and sending the drugs to be analyzed at the state laboratory. The state lab is located in the Capital 250 miles away, and the procedure should be as cost effective as possible.

6.13 Reread Federal Rule of Evidence 104(a) and (b). Authentication is a preliminary fact question to be decided by the judge. In making her decision, should the judge be able to rely on evidence that would be inadmissible under the rules of evidence? Why or why not?

6.14 FACT INVESTIGATION/DEPOSITION. Plaintiff went to the corner deli and bought a jar of "Mrs. White's" pickled watermelon. Plaintiff alleges she was injured when she ate glass contained in the jar. The jar has a label printed with "Mrs. White's Co." in bold print and "Hand Packaged by Mrs. White's Co." in smaller print. The jar has Owens Glass Co.'s logo stamped on it. Plaintiff sues the owner of the deli and Mrs. White's. Mrs. White's denies that this is one of its jars of watermelon.

    .1 Assume the Federal Rules of Evidence and the Federal Rules of Civil Procedure *do not* apply. Develop a fact investigation plan which will provide you with enough additional evidence to authenticate the jar and its label. Identify the key legal or factual propositions crucial for you to authenticate the evidence. Itemize the specific evidence from witnesses as well as demonstrative and physical evidence you expect to gather. Finally, indicate where and how you should look for this evidence. **Be sure to fill out the joint questionnaire following development of the fact investigation plan.**

.2 What difference would it make if the Federal Rules of Evidence and Civil Procedure apply?

Chapter 7

THE ORIGINAL DOCUMENT RULE

7.1   Consider:

.1 Defendant manufacturer is charged with sewing too many pockets on jackets, in violation of wartime conservation laws. At trial, the prosecutor offers testimony concerning the number of pockets on defendant's jackets. Defendant objects based on the original document rule, claiming the jackets themselves should be produced. What result?

.2 Two parties enter into a written contract. In a subsequent breach of contract action, in order to prove the terms of the contract, does the original document rule apply?

.3 Two parties enter into an oral contract. In a subsequent breach of contract action, to prove the substance of the contract, may one of the parties call her secretary who was present at the negotiation and have him testify as to the terms of the contract?

.4 Assume that in the previous question rather than the secretary testifying, one of the parties had gone back to her office and prepared a memorandum of her recollections of the negotiation and the agreement reached. In the subsequent breach of contract action, to prove the substance of the contract, must the memorandum be produced?

.5 Refer to problem 4.29.1 Instead of introducing the 911 transcript, the prosecutor seeks to have the operator testify about the substance of the conversation. What result?

.6 Defendant is charged with contributing to the delinquency of a minor. The prosecutor has video recordings of defendant and the minor engaged in sexual intercourse. To prove that defendant and the minor engaged in sexual intercourse, must the prosecutor introduce the recordings?

.7 Assume that the same recording as in the previous problem is in the possession of the prosecutor. In a prosecution for the distribution of obscene material (*i.e.*, the video recording of people engaged in sexual intercourse) does the original document rule require the production of the recording?

.8 Refer to problem 4.49 Instead of trying to introduce the lab reports, the prosecutor calls to the stand the lab technician who tested the substance. The lab technician does not bring the lab reports with him. The technician proposes to testify that he tested the drugs in question and that the drugs were cocaine. Defense counsel objects based on the original documents rule. What result?

.9 *Paula v. David and PDG.* Paula claims she received a broken leg in the accident. She calls to the stand her treating physician who will testify that after reviewing X-rays, he set Paula's leg and provided follow-up treatment. Does the original document rule require the production of the hospital X-rays to prove the existence of the broken bone?

.10 In a medical malpractice action, plaintiff claims that the defendant doctor breached the standard of care by his failure to properly read the X-ray that showed a broken leg. Does the original document rule require production of the X-ray?

.11 Refer to problem 5.13. Assuming Dr. Edmond's testimony is admitted, does the original document rule require production of the document he relied upon?

.12 Buyer and seller have a dispute as to whether the purchase price of an item has been paid. Buyer has a receipt for the $100, but has left it at home. Buyer wishes to testify that he paid the final $100 installment. Seller objects based on the original document rule. What result?

.13 Assume that in the previous question the Buyer wishes to testify, "I paid the $100, in fact I have a receipt that says, 'Received $100' and is signed by Seller." Seller objects based on the original document rule. What result?

.14 Refer to problem 7.1.6. The prosecutor has still photographs of the defendant and the minor engaged in sexual intercourse. A police officer gets on the stand to testify that he has seen the photographs. He then begins to describe the content of the photographs. Defendant objects based on the original document rule. What result? Assume the police officer offered a print of the photograph, and defendant objected, claiming that the negatives of the print were required. What result?

.15 Defendant is charged with production and sale of counterfeit tennis shoes. The shoes allegedly say "Converse" on them, and are designed to look like Converse tennis shoes. A Converse investigator takes the stand and testifies that he was approached by defendant and offered a shoe that he attempts to describe. Defendant's counsel objects. How should the court rule?

.16 In an action for conversion of an automobile, plaintiff seeks to testify as to the serial number on the car? Does the original document rule require production of the car?

.17 Defendant is charged with rustling cattle belonging to the Circle O Ranch. A police officer seeks to describe the brand found on the cattle in defendant's possession as the same as the Circle O's. Does the original document rule require production of the cattle before the police officer can describe the brand?

.18 Refer to problem 4.48.2. Gina's attorney objects based on the original document rule. What result?

7.2 A local homeowner seeks to challenge a zoning change. State law provides that to have standing to challenge a zoning change you must be a property owner within the jurisdiction seeking to make the change. When the homeowner takes the stand to testify that he does indeed own real estate, the opponent objects based on the fact that the owner's deed is required under the original document rule. How should the judge rule?

7.3 Defendant is charged with conspiracy to commit the murder of her business partner. To prove motive, the government calls the intended victim to the stand who testifies that he and the defendant had taken out key-person life insurance policies in the amount of $50,000 in the event either of them died. Defense counsel objects based on the original document rule. What result?

7.4 In each of the following instances, what is the original document?

.1 A local newspaper printed a story in which a reporter wrote that, in a speech at a public forum, a law student called a law professor incompetent. The law professor sues the student in a defamation action. At trial, the law professor calls a witness to testify about the student's reference to the professor as incompetent. The defendant's counsel objects on the basis of the original document rule, claiming that the professor must produce the newspaper article. What ruling? Suppose the professor sued the reporter. Would the original document rule apply? What if he sued the newspaper?

.2 In a breach of contract action, the offer was sent by FAX machine. The acceptance was sent by mail. In order to establish the terms of the contract, what copies are required by the original document rule?

.3 Assume in the previous problem that the offer was actually mailed to the other party, with the offeror retaining a photocopy in her files. May the offeror use the photocopy to meet the original document rule?

.4 The suit involves a breach of contract for the sale of a home. A form contract was used, with the real estate agent filling in each of the blanks. Four photocopies of the contract were then made. These four copies, and the one filled in by the agent, were independently signed by the parties. In a suit for specific performance of the real estate contract, which of these five copies is an original? Assume the copies were not independently signed, but the first was signed and then the other four copies were made. Does this change your answer?

7.5 Refer to problem 7.1.6. The prosecutor seeks to introduce an enlarged photograph extracted from the video recording. Defendant objects based on the original document rule. What result?

7.6   If under Federal Rule 1003 duplicates are as fully admissible as originals, is there any difference between an original and a duplicate?

7.7   WITNESS EXAMINATION. *State v. Duffy.* Assume Duffy signed his statement to the police. Officer Gorham is on the stand. The following takes place:

> By the Prosecutor:
>
> Q: After you gave the defendant his *Miranda* rights at the police station, did he talk to you?
>
> A: Yes.
>
> Q: What did he say?
>
> By Defendant's Counsel: Objection, your honor, best evidence.
>
> Q: That's quite all right, your honor, I'll rephrase the question. Officer Gorham, did the defendant sign a statement after talking to you?
>
> A: Yes.
>
> Q: And what did that statement say?
>
> By Defendant's Counsel: Objection, your honor, best evidence.

What is the proper ruling on defense counsel's two objections?

7.8   The Internal Revenue Service brings suit to collect taxes. Under applicable law, the statute of limitations bars the suit unless the taxpayer executed a waiver extending the limitations period.

> **.1** The taxpayer denies the existence of a waiver. The IRS attempts to use secondary evidence to prove the existence of a waiver signed by the taxpayer, claiming its copy of the two originals was destroyed following standard IRS procedures. May the IRS use secondary evidence? Assuming secondary evidence is permitted, what type of evidence would be admissible?
>
> **.2** Suppose the taxpayer admits that a waiver was signed, but disputes its terms, claiming the waiver does not apply in this suit. Also, assume the taxpayer is divorced and claims that his former spouse has all his original tax records. Would this new information affect your answer in the previous problem? Is there any additional information you need?

7.9   In a breach of contract action, plaintiff seeks to introduce oral testimony concerning the contents of the contract. Plaintiff claims that his copy of the contract was destroyed in a fire and that the defendant has the only other original. Defendant objects, claiming plaintiff failed to serve a subpoena duces tecum for the contract.

.1 What standard of proof should the trial court use in determining the unavailability of the document plaintiff says was destroyed by fire?

.2 Should plaintiff be prohibited from providing oral testimony because of her failure to serve a subpoena duces tecum?

.3 Assume the defendant denies the contract was ever executed. How should the existence or nonexistence of the document be determined?

.4 Assume Defendant does produce a contract, but plaintiff asserts that a material term has been changed. May plaintiff testify to her recollection as to what she claims were the terms of the contract?

7.10   Defendant is on trial for bribery and conspiracy to commit bribery. It is alleged that he and three other individual put together a scheme to bribe a member of Congress. To help prove the conspiracy, the prosecutor subpoenaed the telephone records of the defendant. The records show over 500 calls to the alleged coconspirators over a two month period. The telephone records are on file in the prosecutor's office and have been made available to the defendant. Prior to calling her first witness, the prosecutor seeks to introduce a summary of the telephone calls. What grounds exist for the defendant to object?

7.11   Peter is the owner of several rent controlled housing units. Peter brings suit against the City Housing Authority (CHA) under 42 U.S.C. § 1983, alleging that CHA discriminates against him on the basis of race. He maintains that CHA allows lower rents to be maintained on his apartments than on the apartments of people of other races. CHA, in order to rebut Peter's claim, did a survey of 150 controlled rental units in the area contiguous to Peter's units. The survey consisted of reviewing contracts between CHA and the owners, personally interviewing one-half the owners, and on-site visits of the premises. The findings of the investigation were summarized in a document containing the name of the owner, location of the rental units, race of the owner, and rent charged for each unit. The actual notes of the investigators were routinely destroyed following compilation of the data. The summary shows that Peter receives above average rent. What grounds exist for Peter to object?

7.12   Refer to problem 5.8.1. Assume that Dr. Duke claims he read the lab report as soon as it was completed, which happened to be two days after treating Mr. Perry.

.1 Mr. Perry seeks to call a witness who will testify that the lab report was dated on the same day that Perry went to the emergency room. Dr. Duke objects based on the original document rule, claiming that the lab slip must be accounted for. What result?

.2 Assume that, without accounting for the unavailability of the lab report, Mr. Perry seeks to introduce the following portion of the transcript of Dr. Duke's deposition.

Q: What date was on the lab report?

A: I'm not sure of the date, but I know it was the same day he came into the emergency room.

Defense counsel objects based on hearsay and best evidence. What result?

.3 Assume that, without accounting for the unavailability of the lab report, Mr. Perry calls a nurse who will testify that she heard Dr. Duke tell a colleague, "Of course, the difficulty is that the lab report says the test was done on the day of Perry's injury." Defense counsel objects based on hearsay and best evidence. What result?

Chapter 8

REAL, ILLUSTRATIVE, EXPERIMENTAL AND SCIENTIFIC EVIDENCE

8.1 WITNESS EXAMINATION. *State v. Duffy.* Introduce the briefcase seized at the crime scene by calling and examining any witnesses you believe necessary.

8.2 *Paula v. David and PDG.* Paula seeks to introduce a photograph of the intersection where the accident occurred. The photograph was taken by the police the day after the accident. The police photographer is not available. Discuss the methods available to introduce the photograph and the use to which the photograph may be put.

8.3 WITNESS EXAMINATION. *State v. Duffy.* Assume the bank had a closed circuit video camera operating during the robbery. Be prepared to call and examine any witnesses you believe necessary to introduce the digital recording showing the robbery.

8.4 WITNESS EXAMINATION. Refer to 7.1.6. Introduce the recordings in the contributing to the delinquency action by calling and examining any witnesses you believe necessary. Would the examination differ if the lawsuit involved the pornography charge in problem 7.1.7?

8.5 WITNESS EXAMINATION. *Paula v. David and PDG.* Wanda will testify that just before the accident she left the Peking Restaurant, two doors down from the southeast corner of Libbie and Grove. As she left the restaurant, she turned right and walked toward her car that was parked on the street approximately 30 feet from the northeast corner of Libbie and Grove. As she approached the intersection, she stopped to wait for the light to change. As she waited, she looked up and saw David's truck traveling south on Grove. She first saw the truck as it passed the intersection of Grove and Maple. She then looked to her left and saw Paula's car traveling east on Libbie. As Paula's car entered the intersection, David's truck struck her left rear. Conduct the direct examination of Wanda eliciting this testimony and using the diagram found in Appendix C. Assume the diagram is *not* drawn to scale. Also for David, prepare to object to the use of the diagram. What difference would it make if the drawing were to scale? Could a blackboard be used? If she is allowed to use a diagram or the blackboard, should the jury be allowed to take the diagram back to the jury room when it deliberates? If the court allows use of the blackboard, how will you preserve the diagram for appeal?

8.6 In a personal injury action involving an airplane crash, plaintiff was severely injured and became a quadriplegic. Plaintiff hired a professional video photographer to produce a DVD. The DVD, 30 minutes long, shows "a day in the life" of plaintiff beginning from her waking up in the morning until she goes to sleep at night. Defense counsel objects to showing the DVD to the jury. What ruling?

8.7 *State v. Duffy.* Assume Arlo will not take the witness stand. He does, however, want the jury see his hands and eyes. Contrary to the Sherry Van Donk's statement, Arlo's eyes are brown. Also, his left hand has a small tattoo that is not referred to in any of the witnesses' statements or testimony. The prosecutor objects. What result?

8.8 FACT INVESTIGATION. *State v. Duffy.* In conducting your investigation as defense counsel, Arlo has identified an eyewitness that places him in Clinton, his mother's hometown, at 12:00 noon on the day of the robbery. You now want to establish that if Arlo was in Clinton a 12:00 noon, he could not have robbed the bank at 1:30 p.m. To do this you want your private investigator to determine how long it takes to drive from Arlo's mother's house to the bank. What instructions should you provide the investigator?

8.9 In a murder prosecution, the prosecutor offers expert testimony that indicated the victim died 90 minutes before the police arrived on the scene. This expert testimony is based, in part, on a comparison of the victim's body temperature and the air temperature of 45 degrees Fahrenheit. A cup of ice cream was found at the scene of a murder. Its location in relation to the body would allow the inference that the victim was eating the ice cream when he was killed. When the police arrived, the ice cream was completely melted.

.1 To prove the time of death was later than that testified to by the prosecution's expert, defendant offers the testimony of his private investigator who will, if allowed, testify that he took the same kind and amount of ice cream to his office and it took two hours to melt. The prosecution objects. What result?

.2 Assume that instead of having the private investigator testify, the defendant seeks to have a cup of the same kind and amount of ice cream introduced into evidence and then time how long it takes to melt in the courtroom. The prosecution objects. What result?

8.10 *Paula v. David and PDG.* Marla Graff, counsel for PDG, seeks to call as a witness an automotive engineering professor from a large state university. The professor will offer to show a computer-generated simulation of the accident in question. The professor has developed a computer program that allows him to recreate automobile accidents, including a visual representation of the accident as "seen" from various vantage points, including the drivers' seats of the vehicles involved in the accident. The professor will testify that he developed the computer program as part of his research into automotive safety. He will further state that although he has never testified at a trial, he has been using the program and various improvements in the program in consulting with auto manufacturers for the past five years. The professor, if allowed, will state that in his opinion, and as seen by his computer-generated simulation, David could not have caused the accident. Should the professor's testimony and computer-generated simulation be admitted into evidence?

8.11   Reconsider problems 5.10 and 5.11.

Chapter 9

RULES OF RELEVANCE

A. Subsequent Remedial Measures

9.1 In which, if any, of the following circumstances is the evidence admissible?

.1 Terrence, a tenant, slips and falls on the top two steps of a common stairway in his apartment building. Terrence sues Larry for personal injury, alleging the stairs were rotted. Two days after the accident, Larry, who admits being the landlord, replaced the rotted, now broken, stairs.

.2 In the same action as 9.1.1, the tenant wishes to introduce evidence that two days before the accident the landlord replaced the bottom two steps on the staircase.

.3 *Paula v. David and PDG.* To help prove damages, Paula seeks to show that PDG paid $1,500 to repair damage to its truck caused by the accident.

.4 Plaintiff sues a small shop owner for a slip and fall on a sidewalk. Applicable law provides that the shop owner is liable for upkeep on the sidewalk. Plaintiff seeks to introduce evidence that two days after the accident, workers from the city repaired the sidewalk.

.5 In the same action as 9.1.1, Larry claims he is not liable because he does not own the building.

.6 In a personal injury action, plaintiff alleges that defendant's brakes were defective. Defendant was not the owner of the car, but plaintiff alleges defendant was authorized by the owner to drive the car. Defendant denies he was driving, claiming he was the passenger and that the driver died in the accident. Plaintiff seeks to introduce evidence that defendant had the brakes on the car fixed after the accident.

9.2 *Paula v. David and PDG.* Paula seeks to introduce evidence that two days after the accident PDG fired David. Is this evidence admissible?

9.3 Able, a building contractor, purchased $550,000 worth of gold tinted window glass from defendant glass manufacturer. Upon delivery and installation of the windows, it was apparent that the color of the windows was not uniform, thus creating a checkerboard appearance. Able sues the manufacturer for breach of contract. At trial, Able wishes to introduce evidence that the defendant changed its manufacturing process so that mistakes in color cannot now happen. Defendant objects on the basis that this testimony concerns a subsequent remedial measure. What ruling?

9.4 In a strict liability action, plaintiff sues the manufacturer of a snow blowing machine because one year ago plaintiff's hand was severed by the machine. Plaintiff claims the machine should have been built so that the blades would automatically stop turning when the operator's hands were removed from the push handle.

> **.1** Plaintiff seeks to introduce evidence that following his injury the defendant changed its design so that the blades automatically stop when the operator's hands are removed from the push handle. Defendant objects. What result?

> **.2** Plaintiff seeks to introduce a later model snow blowing machine, built by a different manufacturer that contains the automatic shut down design. Defendant objects. What ruling?

> **.3** Assume plaintiff purchased his snow blower three years ago. Two years ago defendant changed its design to include the automatic shut-design. Defendant objects. What ruling? Would it make a difference if the design change had been motivated by an accident similar to plaintiff's?

> **.4** Assume defendant countered that while such a design was feasible, any advantages in safety that were gained were offset by disadvantages of such a design. Would this affect your answers?

9.5 Refer to problem 1.6. On the issue of punitive damages, defendant wishes to introduce evidence that after plaintiff's complaints it instituted a large scale education and training program as a means of mitigating such complaints in the future. Plaintiff objects. What result?

9.6 If evidence is inadmissible as a subsequent remedial measure, should details concerning the remedial measure be discoverable?

9.7 Is not feasibility of precautionary measures an issue in all negligence actions? If so, does this exception swallow the rule?

B. Compromise and Offers to Compromise

9.8 *Paula v. David and PDG.* Paula seeks to testify that immediately after the accident, David got out of his truck and said, "I'm sorry. Don't call your insurance company or anything. I'll pay to have your car fixed." David objects, citing Federal Rule of Evidence 408. What ruling?

9.9 Refer to problem 5.8.1.

.1 Perry wishes to introduce a letter sent to his attorney from Duke's attorney. Assume the letter contains the following statement. "As stated in our recent telephone conversation, Dr. Duke denies any negligence on his part. We certainly hope to avoid a trial, however, and are, therefore, willing to pay Mr. Perry $150,000." Defense counsel objects to the introduction of the letter. What ruling?

.2 Suppose instead the letter said, "As I stated on the phone, Dr. Duke should have read the culture within 48 hours, but that did not cause the injury. We certainly hope to avoid a trial, and are, therefore, willing to pay Mr. Perry $150,000." At trial can Perry introduce the letter to show that Dr. Duke did not read the report within 48 hours?

.3 Suppose instead the letter said, "As I said on the phone, Dr. Duke should have read the culture within 48 hours, and I agree that a jury could return one million in damages. But, the fact remains that to get that you'll have to sue. We certainly hope to avoid a trial, and are, therefore, willing to pay Mr. Perry $150,000." Defense counsel objects to the introduction of the letter. What ruling?

.4 Assume that any one of the above letters was sent and that the $150,000 was accepted by Perry. Perry, however, failed to receive the $150,000. In a suit to enforce the agreement to pay the $150,000, may Perry introduce the letter?

.5 Assume Perry has settled his lawsuit against Dr. Duke, but still has a suit pending against the hospital. Perry seeks to introduce the fact that Duke has settled. The hospital objects based on Federal Rule 408. What ruling?

.6 Assume Perry has settled his lawsuit against Dr. Duke, but still has a suit pending against the hospital. Duke testifies for Perry against the hospital at the trial. The hospital then seeks to introduce the fact that Duke has settled. Perry objects based on Federal Rule 408. What ruling?

.7 Plaintiff was involved in two automobile accidents. The first accident occurred in August, and the second in November. The claims arising from the August accident ultimately were settled. Plaintiff files a motion in limine to exclude any reference to the settlement of the August accident claim. Defendant maintains she intends to use the evidence of settlement of the first case to demonstrate bias, as plaintiff "has every reason to minimize his injuries from the August accident, because he had already settled his claim with regard to that accident." How should the court rule?

9.10 Refer to problem 5.8.1.

.1 Assume that Dr. Duke attended a settlement meeting with his attorney, opposing counsel, and Mr. Perry. During that meeting, Duke stated, "I did not read the lab report within 24 hours, but that did not cause the permanent damage suffered by Mr. Perry. The chainsaw did that." On direct examination, Dr. Duke claims he read the report within 24 hours. In rebuttal, Perry seeks to testify to Duke's statement. Duke's attorney objects. What result?

.2 Assume that Dr. Duke's lawyer attended a settlement meeting with Perry's lawyer. Duke was not present, but Perry was present. Duke's lawyer said during the meeting that, "Dr. Duke did not read the lab report within 24 hours, but that did not cause the permanent damage suffered by Mr. Perry." On direct examination, Dr. Duke claims he read the report within 24 hours. In rebuttal, Perry seeks to testify to Duke's statement. Duke's attorney objects. What result?

C. Payment of Medical and Similar Expenses

9.11   *Paula v. David and PDG.* Refer to problem 9.8. Assume, however, that David said, "Don't worry, I'll pay your medical bills." David objects, citing Federal Rule of Evidence 409. What ruling?

9.12   Parker was involved in an automobile accident, broke his leg and was required to be out of work for nine months. At the time of the accident he was working as a deck hand on a merchant ship. During the nine-month period, Parker received maintenance payments from the ship's company pursuant to a union contract. After the nine months Parker was able to return to work, but was ordered by his doctor to do only light work, part-time.

When he went back to his employer, the employer told Parker to go to a company owned private hunt club and do part-time, light landscape work. During this period, he continued to receive maintenance payments consistent with part-time work. After several weeks, Parker re-injured his leg.

The employer has denied continued maintenance payments claiming Parker is not covered by the seaman contract because he was not a seaman at the time of the leg re-injury. In a suit to recover, among other things, maintenance payments, Parker seeks to introduce evidence that during the first nine months he did not work, and for the several weeks he worked part-time, the company made maintenance payments. The company objects. What ruling?

D. Pleas, Plea Discussions, and Related Statements

9.13   Defendant is charged with aggravated battery, pleads guilty, and is sentenced to two years. The victim then sues the same defendant for civil assault and battery.

.1 Is the guilty plea entered in the criminal action admissible in the civil action? If the plea is admissible, for what purpose would it be admissible?

.2 Assume that instead of pleading guilty, the defendant pleaded *nolo contendere*. Would your answer change?

9.14   *State v. Duffy.* Assume that at the time of Arlo's arrest he was taken to the police station, given his *Miranda* warnings, but did not request an attorney.

.1 During questioning, one of the police officers stated, "Arlo, fess up now, and we'll see what we can do with the judge. It will probably save you five years in prison." Arlo then admitted robbing the bank. At trial, Arlo denies having robbed the bank and seeks to exclude his confession to the police. What ruling?

.2 Suppose in problem 9.14.1 the person questioning Arlo was an assistant district attorney. Would that affect your answer? What if the discussions with the district attorney came after Arlo was indicted?

E. Liability Insurance

9.15   Consider:

.1 *Paula v. David and PDG.* David, after running into Paula, got out of his truck, ran up to her and said "don't worry, the company's insurance will cover this." Defendant objects when plaintiff seeks to testify to this statement. What ruling?

.2 Plaintiff was run over by a moped driven by David. In a personal injury action, plaintiff sues Olivia, alleging she is the owner of the moped and she negligently entrusted it to David. Olivia claims she does not own the moped. Can plaintiff introduce testimony that Olivia insures the moped?

.3 *Paula v. David and PDG.* An insurance adjuster testifies on behalf of the defendant as to the extent of damage to plaintiff's car. Can the insurance adjuster be asked on cross-examination, "Isn't it true you work for the company insuring defendant?"

9.16   Refer to problem 1.3. Defendants seek to exclude evidence that the government may indemnify defendants if they lose the lawsuit.

F. Habit; Routine Practice; Introduction to Character

9.17   *Paula v. David and PDG.* Paula seeks to prove that David ran the red light at the intersection. David, in order to prove that he did not run the light seeks to introduce the following testimony. Indicate whether the following testimony is admissible.

.1 David will testify that he always stops at red lights.

.2 David will testify that he always stops at stop signs.

.3 David will call a witness who will testify that she has known David for 20 years and that he always stops at red lights.

.4 David will call a witness who will testify that on ten separate occasions he was out in his yard working when David drove by his house and stopped at the red light on the corner.

.5 David will call ten separate witnesses who will each testify that they have ridden with David on ten separate occasions and that on the occasion they rode with him he stopped at all red lights.

Is your answer affected by whether there are eyewitnesses to the intersection collision?

9.18   Pam alleges she was injured by an allergic reaction to Swine Flu vaccine. She sues the health center that provided the immunization. The health center defends based on a consent form signed by Pam. The health center, however, cannot find a copy of the form. Because it immunized 500 people in the six day period surrounding Pam's immunization, no one at the center has any personal knowledge of Pam's immunization. The health center seeks to call its medical director to testify that it is the policy of the center that whenever Swine Flu vaccine is administered the patient is informed of the risks and signs a consent form indicating an awareness of the risk. Pam's attorney objects. What ruling?

9.19   Witness Examination. *State v. Duffy.* Priscilla Duffy takes the stand and testifies as follows:

By Defense Counsel

Q: Tell us your name.

A: Priscilla Duffy.

Q: Where do you live?

A: Elm St., Clinton, Columbia.

Q: Could you tell us what is your relationship to Arlo?

A: I'm his mother.

Q: Directing your attention to June 1, Yr-0, where were you that day?

A: At home.

Q: How do you remember?

A: I'm always a home. I broke my hip two years ago and I don't get around very well and only go some place if someone comes to get me, like that nice man you sent.

By Prosecutor: Objection, your honor. Lack of firsthand knowledge.

.1 What ruling?

Q: Did you have a visitor June 1?

A: I would think so. It was the first of the month and Arlo helps write my bills.

By Prosecutor: Objection, your honor, irrelevant.

.2 What ruling?

Q: What time did he arrive?

A: Probably around 10:30, in the morning.

By Prosecutor: Objection, your honor, irrelevant, move to strike the answer.

By Defendant's Counsel: Your honor, if I may rephrase my questions?

By the Court: Yes.

.3 Complete defense counsel's questions eliciting, evidence of the times of arrival and departure of Arlo on June 1, Yr-0.

9.20   Phoebe was injured when her airplane seat belt broke on landing and she was thrown forward. Phoebe sued the manufacturer of the airplane. The manufacturer defended on the ground that the seat belt was improperly repaired by the airline, causing the belt to fray and eventually sever. In an attempt to establish this defense, the manufacturer seeks to introduce evidence that an inspection of the airline's six planes showed that five of the six had a total of 191 frayed seat belts. Plaintiff objects. What ruling?

9.21   In which, if any, of the following circumstances is the evidence admissible?

.1 Theft prosecution. On the issue of whether defendant robbed the particular home in question, evidence that the defendant has robbed three other homes.

.2 *Paula v. David and PDG.* Paula seeks to introduce testimony that David always carried a beer in his truck during working hours and that at some time during his shift he would drink the beer.

.3 *Paula v. David and PDG.* Paula seeks to prove that David was drunk at the time of the accident. To do so, Paula seeks to introduce evidence that David has four prior convictions for public drunkenness during the past three years.

.4 Paula v. David and PDG. To show that he was driving carefully at the time of the accident, David seeks to testify that he is a careful driver.

G. Character Evidence for Substantive Purposes

9.22 *Paula v. David and PDG.* Paula sues PDG on a theory of negligent entrustment.

.1 At trial Paula seeks to introduce testimony that David has the reputation within the company as a reckless driver. Defense counsel objects. What ruling? Could Paula offer the testimony of a witness who will state that he has ridden with David on two separate occasions and that on both of those occasions David drove recklessly?

.2 Suppose Paula was killed and defendant is sued in a wrongful death action. Defendants seek to introduce testimony that Paula was a lazy individual who had lost two jobs in the last three years. Plaintiff's counsel objects. What ruling?

9.23 *Donato v. Donato.* Paul takes the stand and testifies, that

.1 Gina is an immoral woman. Gina's counsel objects. What ruling?

.2 Gina has committed adultery. Gina's counsel objects. What ruling?

9.24 In a prosecution for illegal possession of a firearm by a convicted felon, the prosecutor seeks to introduce the defendant's prior felony convictions. They consist of two armed robberies and a sodomy conviction. Defense counsel objects. What ruling?

9.25 *State v. Duffy.* Arlo calls the following witnesses to testify as indicated. Assume each witness is the first witness called by Arlo in his defense. The prosecutor objects to each. What ruling?

.1 Arlo calls Beatrice who will testify that she believes Arlo is a truthful individual.

.2 Arlo calls his mother who will testify that in his entire life Arlo has never stolen anything.

.3 Arlo calls a person he met after his arrest who will testify that, in his opinion, Arlo is a law-abiding person.

.4 Arlo calls his neighbor for the past two years who will testify that in his opinion Arlo is a law-abiding person.

.5 Arlo himself takes the stand and testifies on direct, "I'm just not the kind of guy who would rob a bank."

9.26 In criminal prosecution for income tax evasion, David Daniels, defendant, calls to the stand a witness who will testify as follows. For each of the following objections, indicate whether the court ruled appropriately.

Q: Do you know the defendant?

A: Yes.

Q: How long have you known him?

A: Four years.

Q: In what settings have you known the defendant?

A: We work together.

Q: Have you had any opportunity to observe his truthfulness?

A: Plenty of times.

Q: Could you tell us about those times?

.1 By the Prosecutor: Objection, your honor.

By the Court: Sustained

Q: Do you have an opinion of Mr. Daniel's truthfulness?

A: Yes.

Q: What is that opinion?

A: He is a truthful person.

On cross-examination the prosecutor asks:

Q: Did you know the defendant was arrested for perjury three years ago?

.2 By Defense Counsel: Objection.

By the Court: Overruled, you may answer.

A: No.

Q: Have you heard the defendant was convicted of armed robbery just last year?

.3 By Defense Counsel: Objection

By the Court: Sustained

After the defense rests, the prosecutor in rebuttal calls to the stand a co-worker of the defendant. After laying a foundation that indicates the witness has worked with the defendant for the past four years, the prosecutor asks:

Q: Have you and other workers ever discussed the defendant's truthfulness?

A: Oh, yes, on numerous occasions.

Q: What have they said?

.4 By Defense Counsel: Objection, hearsay and improper character evidence.

By the Court: Sustained.

Q: Have you and the other workers ever discussed the defendant's truthfulness?

A: Again, many times.

Q: Do you know defendant's reputation at work for truthfulness?

A: Certainly.

Q: What is that reputation?

.5 By Defense Counsel: Objection.

By the Court: Sustained.

Q: Do you have an opinion as to the defendant's truthfulness?

A: Yes.

Q: What is that opinion?

.6 By Defense Counsel: Objection.

By the Court: Overruled.

Q: You may answer.

A: He's a liar.

9.27   Defendant, Alice, is charged with assault with intent to commit murder in the shooting of her former boyfriend Arnold. Alice claims self-defense. Alice is the only witness for the defense. Which, if any, of the following evidence is admissible?

.1 The prosecutor, in her case-in-chief, seeks to introduce evidence that Alice's reputation is that she is a violent person.

.2 The prosecutor, in her case-in-chief, seeks to introduce evidence that Arnold's reputation is that he is a peaceful person.

.3 Alice, in defense, seeks to testify that two years ago Arnold assaulted a police officer.

.4 Alice then seeks to testify that Arnold is an aggressive and violent person.

.5 Alice next seeks to testify that twice in the past year Arnold has assaulted her.

.6 Alice next testifies that she shot Arnold when he attacked her after breaking into her apartment in a fit of rage over their recent separation.

May the prosecutor in rebuttal call a long time friend of Arnold's who will testify that Arnold was a peaceful person?

.7 Assume the judge allows the testimony in 9.27.4. May the prosecutor in rebuttal call a long time friend of Arnold's who will testify that Arnold was a peaceful person?

.8 Assume the judge allows the testimony in 9.27.4. May the prosecutor now, in rebuttal, introduce testimony that Alice is a violent person?

.9 Would your answer to any of these questions change if Arnold had died and Alice was on trial for murder?

9.28 Defendants, Betty and Carol, are charged with assault with a deadly weapon and assault resulting in serious bodily injury. It is alleged that defendants attacked Vera with a baseball bat. The defendants are on trial together. Each defendant is represented by separate counsel, but each claim self-defense.

.1 The prosecutor calls Vera to testify. On cross-examination, Betty's lawyer asks Vera, "It's true, is it not, that you have a reputation in the community in which you live for violence?" The prosecutor's objection to the question is overruled and Vera says, "absolutely not." Betty then asks Vera, "Isn't it true that a year ago you hit your neighbor, Laura, on the head with brass knuckles?" The prosecutor objects to this question and renews his objection to the original reputation question. What argument should the prosecutor make to convince the judge to sustain the objections to both questions?

.2 In her defense, Betty has Laura testify that Vera has a reputation in the community as a violent person. In rebuttal, the prosecutor calls Dawyne, a police officer, who testifies that both defendants Betty and Carol have reputations in the community as a "prone to violence." Carol's lawyer objects. What is the correct ruling?

9.29 Defendant is on trial for possession with intent to distribute cocaine. Pursuant to a lawful search, the police discovered in a bedroom in defendant's house a significant amount of cocaine along with related paraphernalia and money. Defendant denies any knowledge of the drugs, claiming that a friend was staying with him and using that particular bedroom. The prosecutor seeks to introduce the following testimony. Is it admissible?

.1 The defendant on previous occasions was seen using cocaine.

.2 Three weeks before the search, defendant sold cocaine to an undercover police officer at a night club.

.3 Two hours before the search, defendant sold cocaine to an undercover policeman in defendant's kitchen.

9.30 In which of the following circumstances is evidence of the crime or underlying acts admissible?

.1 *State v. Duffy.* Arlo defends on the basis that he was under hypnotic suggestion to rob the bank. The prosecutor seeks to introduce a prior felony conviction of Arlo for armed robbery of a bank.

.2 *State v. Duffy.* Assume Arlo was arrested a few minutes after the robbery of the bank. The prosecutor wishes to introduce testimony of the arresting officer that when Arlo was arrested he was driving a stolen car.

.3 Refer to problem 1.4. Is testimony concerning the numerous conspiracies to murder, murders and conspiracy to kidnap and kidnappings excluded under Rule 404(b)?

.4 *State v. Duffy.* Assume Arlo is arrested for robbing a second bank three weeks after robbing the First Investors Savings Bank. The manner in which the second robbery was committed was exactly the same manner as the robbery of First Investors. May the prosecutor introduce evidence of the second bank robbery in Arlo's trial for the robbery of First Investors?

.5 Defendant is charged with the robbing drug dealers and requiring them to strip naked. The prosecutor seeks to have defendant's cousin testify that he and defendant once robbed a group of people. While defendant held a gun during this robbery, the cousin beat them up and made them strip naked. One person was forced to ride away on a bike naked. Defense counsel objects. What result?

.6 *State v. Duffy.* The prosecutor seeks to introduce evidence that around noon on the day First Investors was robbed Arlo also got in a fist fight with his neighbor.

.7 Assuming any of the evidence in problems 9.30.5 is admissible, what should be the prosecutor's burden of persuasion in establishing the other act or crime?

.8 Assume the defendant had been acquitted of criminal liability for the crimes or acts in problems 9.30.5. Would your answer change?

H. Sex Offense Cases

9.31 Defendant is charged with rape. Pursuant to Federal Rule of Evidence 412, the court holds a hearing to determine the admissibility of the following evidence. Prepare to argue for and against its admissibility. Defendant seeks to

.1 cross-examine the victim regarding two other men with whom she has had sex.

.2 introduce opinion testimony that the victim is unchaste.

.3 introduce reputation evidence that the victim is unchaste.

.4 cross-examine the victim regarding the fact that she had sex with the defendant approximately one year before the alleged rape.

.5 cross-examine the victim regarding the fact that the victim had sex with the defendant one week before the alleged rape.

9.32 Defendant is charged with rape of his thirteen-year-old niece. Defendant seeks to introduce evidence that on several prior occasions, the niece made rape charges against family members, only subsequently to withdraw the charges. The prosecutor objects under Federal Rule of Evidence 412. What ruling? Suppose in a pre-trial hearing, the court decides to allow the testimony, may the prosecutor appeal that decision immediately?

9.33 Defendant is on trial for sexual abuse. Defendant seeks to introduce testimony from a police officer that while he was interviewing the victim about the sexual abuse, the victim told him that he (the police officer) was "cute" and asked him if he wanted to "crawl into bed" with her. The prosecution objects. What result?

9.34 Criminal action. The prosecutor alleges the defendant and her partner conspired to extort money from the victim. Defendant is alleged to have manipulated the victim into a sexual relationship and then threatened to reveal the relationship to the victim's spouse unless the victim paid defendant $10,000. The prosecutor seeks to introduce testimony from a third party to the effect that the defendant had a sexual relationship with another person from whom he sought to extort money.

9.35 In problem 9.31, assume the defendant was convicted. In a subsequent civil action involving the same incident, defendant seeks to introduce the evidence contained in problems 9.31.1-.5. What result?

9.36 Refer to problem 1.7. One Plaintiff seeks to exclude evidence of her alleged sexual behavior outside the workplace and alleged sexual comments in the workplace. What result?

9.37 Bruce is charged with rape and child molestation. Prosecutors allege that Bruce, 19, beat and forcibly raped H.S., a 12-year-old girl. Bruce claims that H.S. consented to have sexual intercourse with him. The incident allegedly took place following high school basketball game when Bruce encouraged H.S. to take a walk with him to an isolated spot behind the high school building. H.S. told police that immediately after the incident Bruce threatened her not to tell anyone what happened. Ten days before trial, the government gave notice to defense counsel that it intended to call Bruce's cousin, R.M., to testify at trial. If permitted, R.M. will testify that when she was 13-years-old, Bruce forcibly sexually assaulted her in his car and later claimed that she had consented. This incident led to a conviction for child molestation against Bruce. Defense counsel objects to the relevancy of R.M.'s testimony and the prosecutor cites Federal Rules of Evidence 413 and 414 as the basis for admitting the evidence.

.1 Is R.M.'s testimony admissible? Does the fact that the government provided notice of its intent to have R.M. testify only 10 days before trial effect the testimony's admissibility?

.2 Assume there had not been conviction of Bruce for his attack on R.M., would that affect the admissibility of R.M.'s testimony? What if the conviction occurred 12 years ago?

.3 Assume H.S. was 19 at the time of the alleged rape, would that affect the admissibility of R.M.'s testimony?

.4 As part of his defense, Bruce attempts to introduce evidence of a previous sexual assault accusation made by H.S. several years earlier against Chris, a teenage friend of Bruce's. Chris committed suicide before the H.S.' accusation against him could be matter could be adjudicated. Is evidence of the allegedly prior false accusation admissible?

.5 In addition to relying on Federal Rules 413 or 414, what argument could the prosecutor make to support the admissibility of R.M.'s testimony?

9.38   Plaintiff brought suit against defendant, her former guidance counselor, claiming she was sexually harassed and abused her while she was a high school student in the Elk Lake School District. At the time of the alleged harassment, plaintiff was 17-years-old. Defendant was 34-years-old. Plaintiff sought damages from defendant in federal district court claiming violations of 42 U.S.C. § 1983 and state tort law. Plaintiff entered the Elk Lake School District high school as a freshman in September 1991. Plaintiff claims that for two years defendant repeatedly sent her letters, roses, cards, and other suggestive correspondence, attempted on numerous occasions to hug and kiss her without her consent.

Plaintiff seeks to introduce the testimony of Karen regarding an incident in which defendant allegedly sexually assaulted Karen. Plaintiff's lawyer seeks to have Karen testify that she had just walked into a school office when defendant allegedly picked her up and threw her over his shoulder. According to Karen, who was wearing a skirt at the time, defendant's hand went up her skirt and touched her in the crotch area while he raised her off the floor. Defendant soon let her down to the floor and the two of them, proceeded to sit down and eat lunch together.

In her deposition, Karen was asked whether defendant's hand "lingered for any period of time." She responded, "I have to say no." In an earlier interview conducted by plaintiff's attorney outside the presence of opposing counsel, Karen, under oath, was asked if defendant had "left his hand for a while, a moment, two moments or so," to which she responded, "Yeah." When asked during her deposition whether she thought the touching was intentional, Karen seemed unsure: "I guess maybe at the time I didn't feel right, but I guess the greater part of me not wanting to think anything was just like, you know, shrugged it off, no big deal."

When asked by the court what sexual assault law was broken if Plaintiff's story were true, plaintiff's counsel cited the following state law:

§ 3126. Indecent assault

(a) Offense defined. — A person who has indecent contact with the complainant or causes the complainant to have indecent contact with the person is guilty of indecent assault if:

(1) the person does so without the complainant's consent;

(2) the person does so by forcible compulsion;

(3) the person does so by threat of forcible compulsion that would prevent resistance by a person of reasonable resolution;

(4) the complainant is unconscious or the person knows that the complainant is unaware that the indecent contact is occurring;

(5) the person has substantially impaired the complainant's power to appraise or control his or her conduct by administering or employing, without the knowledge of the complainant, drugs, intoxicants or other means for the purpose of preventing resistance;

(6) the complainant suffers from a mental disability that renders him or her incapable of consent;

(7) the complainant is less than 13 years of age; or

(8) the complainant is less than 16 years of age and the person is four or more years older than the complainant and the complainant and the person are not married to each other.

§ 3101. Definitions

The following words and phrases when used in this chapter shall have, unless the context clearly indicates otherwise, the meanings given to them in this section:

. . . .

"Indecent contact." Any touching of the sexual or other intimate parts of the person for the purpose of arousing or gratifying sexual desire, in either person.

.1 Defense counsel objects arguing that there has not been the 15 days notice required under Federal Rule of Evidence 415. What is the correct ruling?

.2 Defense counsel objects arguing that Rule 415 does not apply, because there was no sexual assault in this case. How should the court rule?

.3 Assuming notice is proper and that, if plaintiff's testimony is true, defendant's actions constituted sexual assault, true what other arguments should defense counsel make to persuade the judge that the testimony is inadmissible?

Chapter 10

CROSS-EXAMINATION AND IMPEACHMENT

A. Cross-Examination Generally

10.1 Plaintiff brings suit against a missile manufacturer alleging that the manufacturer negligently handled a toxic gas leak causing severe injury to several hundred people, including himself.

> **.1** Plaintiff calls Dr. Brown who testifies that he has examined the plaintiff, and that in his opinion the plaintiff received severe injuries caused by gas leaking from defendant's plant. On cross-examination, defense counsel asks, "Isn't it true that of the 50 people you examined living in plaintiff's neighborhood, plaintiff is the only one having these symptoms?" Plaintiff's counsel objects. What ruling?

> **.2** Defendant calls the plant manager who denies that the gas leaked, saying, "The plant is very safe." On cross-examination, plaintiff's counsel seeks to question the manager concerning other types of gas leaks that have occurred over the past five years. Defense counsel objects. What ruling?

10.2 Refer to problem 9.25. Assume that at least one of the people in the problem other than Arlo was allowed to testify. On cross-examination, the prosecutor asks one question:

> Q: Now, you weren't at the First Investors Savings Bank during the robbery on June 1 of this year, were you?

Defense counsel objects. What ruling?

10.3 *State v. Duffy.* Assume Arlo and his girlfriend Bea are originally charged as coconspirators in the bank robbery. Assume that the charges against Bea are ultimately dropped. Bea, however, is called by the government which requests it be allowed to use leading questions. Should the request be granted?

10.4 Reconsider problems 3.2 to 3.4.

10.5 *State v. Duffy.* The prosecutor calls Sherry Van Donk as a witness and she testifies consistently with her statement to the police. On cross-examination, Arlo's attorney establishes that Sherry has heard of Arlo before and then asks,

"Isn't it true, that Arlo has a reputation as a lawful person." The prosecutor objects. What ruling? As prosecutor, would you object to this question? What are the consequences of allowing the question to be asked?

B. Who Can You Impeach?

10.6   *State v. Duffy.* Shortly after the robbery, Arlo's girlfriend, Bea, was questioned by the FBI. Bea allegedly told the FBI that on the day of the robbery Arlo asked her to "get rid of a gun." At trial the prosecutor calls Bea and begins to question her concerning her statement to the FBI. Defense counsel objects. The prosecutor requests a *voir dire* examination in which he attempts to show that Bea will say Arlo told her to get rid of the gun. During the *voir dire* examination, however, Bea denies Arlo told her to get rid of the gun, and denies having told the FBI that Arlo told her to do it. Assume after the *voir dire* hearing, Bea is again called by the prosecutor. May the prosecutor ask Bea, "Did Arlo ask you to get rid of a gun?" Assuming the prosecutor asks the question and Bea says no, may the prosecutor call the FBI agent to impeach her?

C. Is It A Proper Subject Matter?

10.7   *Paula v. David and PDG.* Assume Wanda takes the stand and testifies to her ties in the community and to the fact that she has a family and a "loving husband." She then testifies that Paula had the green light.

.1 On cross-examination may defense counsel, over plaintiff's objection, ask, "You are having an affair with Arnold Smith, aren't you?"

.2 Does defense counsel need a good faith basis to ask the question in 10.7.1? Suppose the question was, "Are you having an affair with anyone?" Would defense counsel need a good faith basis to ask the question?

.3 Assume there is no objection in problem 10.7.1. The witness denies the affair. Can the defendant call Arnold Smith to the stand to testify that he is having an affair with the witness?

10.8   *State v. Duffy.* Arlo's mother takes the stand and testifies that she remembers Arlo visiting her on June 1, Yr-0, because that was the day she finally received her income tax refund check. May the prosecutor impeach Mrs. Duffy by attempting to prove that she did not receive an income tax refund?

D. Prior Inconsistent Statements

10.9 *State v. Duffy.* Assume that on direct examination Sherry Van Donk described the robber:

.1 as 160 to 180 pounds, 5'10" tall, blue eyes, wearing blue jeans, a green T shirt, and a blue summer jacket.

.2 as 170 pounds, 5'10" tall, blue eyes, and wearing blue jeans.

.3 as 170 pounds, 5'10" tall, blue eyes, with a scar on his left hand, wearing blue jeans, a green T shirt, and a blue summer jacket.

May the defendant properly impeach Sherry using her statement to the police?

10.10 *Paula v. David and PDG.* Assume Wanda was interviewed by an insurance company investigator six months after the accident.

.1 Wanda told the investigator that she did not remember anything, and, therefore, could not make a statement. At trial, Wanda testifies that Paula had the green light. May David impeach Wanda with her statement to the insurance investigator?

.2 Suppose instead that, six months after the accident, Wanda told the investigator that the light was green for David. At trial, Wanda claims she does not remember who had the green light. May the David impeach Wanda with the prior statement?

10.11 Reconsider problem 9.10.

10.12 *Paula v. David and PDG.* Walter testifies at trial that Paula had the green light.

.1 Walter's statement was taken by the police immediately after the accident. In that statement, signed by Walter and witnessed by the officer at the scene, Walter stated that the light was green for David. Impeach Walter using the signed statement. Would the impeachment be different using common law rules rather than the Federal Rules? How would you prove-up the impeaching material?

.2 Walter's statement was taken by the police immediately after the accident. Walter, however, did not sign the statement. In that statement Walter told the officer that the light was green for David. Impeach Walter using the oral statement. Would the impeachment be different using common law rules rather than the Federal Rules? How would you prove-up the impeaching material?

10.13 *State v. Duffy.* Arlo testifies at trial.

.1 Assume the following exchange takes place on direct:

Q: Where were you on June 1, Yr-0?

A: I went to the beach by myself.

Impeach Arlo with a prior inconsistent statement contained in his statement to Officer Gorham, first assuming that Arlo signed the statement he gave to Officer Gorham and then assuming he refused to sign the statement.

.2 Assume Arlo testifies consistently with his unsigned statement. Cross-examine Arlo using his mother's letter dated May 8, Yr-0.

10.14   In a suit over an insurance company's failure to pay a death benefit, plaintiff calls Harold Walker, long time business associate of the deceased. Walker is asked whether he ever heard the deceased mention suicide. Walker says no. Walker is not cross-examined. Two weeks later, during defendant's presentation of evidence, defense counsel calls a witness who testifies that he talked to Walker about six months ago and Walker told him that the deceased had mentioned suicide on a recent business trip. Plaintiff's counsel objects. What ruling? Suppose the trial was in California and Walker lived in New York. Would that affect your answer?

10.15   Office Practice and Procedure. You are an associate in the litigation section of a 35-member law firm. The firm has a general practice, but leans heavily toward plaintiffs' personal injury and corporate work. Your senior partner has given you responsibility for preparing a draft of part of a memorandum outlining a policy on various aspects of the firm's litigation practice.

You have been instructed to draft standard procedures to be used in interviewing any witness who ultimately might prove unfavorable to the firm's position. Specifically, the partner wants to know how interviews should be conducted so as to preserve the information, communicate the information to other members of the firm working on the case, and use the results of the interview on cross-examination of the witness. Be sure to include who should do the interviews, how the interviews should be conducted, and how the interviews should be memorialized. Anticipate any difficulties you see in your recommendations.

10.16   Office Practice and Procedure. You are an associate in the litigation section of a 35-member law firm. The firm has a general practice, though leans heavily toward plaintiffs' personal injury and corporate work. Your senior partner has given you responsibility for preparing a draft of part of a memo outlining a policy on various aspects of the firm's litigation practice.

You have been instructed to draft standard procedures to be used in taking the deposition of any witness you feel ultimately might prove unfavorable to the firm's position. Specifically, the partner wants to know how the deposition should be conducted so as to best use the results on cross-examination of the witness, should such a cross-examination be required. Be sure to include who should do the depositions, how the deposition should be conducted, and any standard statements or questions that might be routinely used. Anticipate any difficulties you see in your recommendations.

E. Bias, Interest, Corruption

10.17 Witness Examination. *State v. Duffy.* Priscilla Duffy takes the witness stand and testifies. Cross-examine her focusing on that portion of her direct examination found in 9.19.

10.18 *Donato v. Donato.* Gina calls to the witness stand the police officer who filed the reports found in problem 4.48. The officer testifies consistently with the reports.

.1 On cross-examination, Paul's attorney asks,

> Q: You do not like Paul Donato, do you?

> A: No.

> Q: You told your partner he was a thief, didn't you?

Gina's lawyer objects based on hearsay. What ruling?

.2 In rebuttal, Paul calls Matthew Vitti to the stand. Vitti seeks to testify that he and Paul coached together in the same basketball league for several years. He will also testify that the police officer who wrote the reports is the president of the league. Two years ago he and Paul attempted to oust the officer from the presidency because of mismanagement. Gina's counsel objects to this testimony. What ruling?

F. Capacity

10.19 *State v. Duffy.* Assume Roy Smith takes the stand and testifies consistently with the police reports.

.1 On cross-examination can Arlo's lawyer establish that Roy is a patient in a mental institution and has been diagnosed as paranoid?

.2 Assume Arlo's lawyer does not cross-examine Roy. In rebuttal, may Arlo call a member of the staff of the hospital to testify that Roy is a patient there? Could the staff member testify as to Roy's diagnosis? Could Arlo introduce expert psychiatric testimony that would explicitly say that because of Roy's mental illness he is not a credible witness? Under what other circumstances might this testimony be relevant?

.3 On cross-examination can Arlo's lawyer ask if Roy wears glasses? If Roy denies wearing glasses, can Arlo introduce a testimony from a hospital aide that Roy wears glasses? Would it affect your answer if Arlo has made a specific allegation that Roy wears glasses, but left them in the hospital on the day of the robbery?

.4 Suppose Roy was in the hospital as a patient in a substance abuse program. Could Arlo bring the existence of the substance abuse out on cross-examination? Would it matter what the substance was?

.5 Reconsider problem 2.5.

G. Convictions

10.20   In a criminal prosecution for filing false income tax returns, a witness is now subject to cross-examination. Under which of the following circumstances may the witness be impeached with his criminal conviction record? Is there any additional information you would like to have? The record is as follows:

Eight year old conviction for income tax evasion (filing false return) (served two years)

Five year old conviction for burglary (served 18 months)

Three year old conviction for drunk and disorderly (fined $50)

One year old conviction for petty larceny (misdemeanor) (served 90 days)

.1 Assume the witness is a friend of the defendant who testifies that in his opinion the defendant is a lawful person.

.2 Assume the defendant is the witness and he testifies that he did not commit the crime.

.3 Assume the witness is a prosecution witness who testifies he was told by the defendant that he, the defendant, had "cheated the government."

.4 Assume that instead of a criminal prosecution, this is a civil action involving a personal injury. The witness has been called by the defendant to testify that the light was green for the defendant. Would your answer in the above situations change?

.5 Would your answer in the above situations change if any of the convictions were the result of pleas of *nolo contendere*?

.6 If any of these convictions can be used, what information concerning the convictions may the cross-examiner elicit? How would the cross-examination take place?

10.21   Defendant is on trial for grand larceny. He is alleged to have shoplifted goods valued at more than $1,000. Defendant has two prior convictions. One prior conviction is for grand larceny, a felony. The other conviction is for petty larceny. The petty larceny conviction involved stealing a sweater by going to the check out and telling the clerk that he wanted to buy the sweater, but that he needed to show it to his wife first. His wife, he said was out at the curb in the car waiting. He then left the store, never to return.

.1 Defendant filed a motion in limine seeking to have the prior conviction excluded for impeachment purposes. The judge refuses to rule on the motion. Why might the judge choose to not rule on the motion? What would the judge's ultimate decision on the admissibility of the evidence likely be?

.2 Assume the judge chooses to rule and denies defendant's motion. What must the defendant do in order to preserve his objection for appeal?

10.22 Assume that in 10.20. the income tax conviction was 11 years old. Under what circumstances, if any, would the conviction be admissible? If defendant had been pardoned for the tax evasion conviction would that change your answer? Would it change your answer if the tax evasion conviction were more recent and still subject to a pending appeal?

10.23 Defendant is charged with conspiracy to sell controlled substances. The prosecutor alleges that the defendant employed children between the ages of 12 and 14 to sell drugs on public school grounds. The prosecutor calls as a witness one of these children who testifies to the defendant's criminal activity. On cross-examination defense counsel seeks to cross-examine the witness based on a juvenile record that includes an adjudication of delinquency for auto theft, and an adjudication for conspiracy to sell drugs. The latter adjudication arose out of the witness's activities with the defendant. May defendant impeach the witness with his juvenile adjudications?

10.24 Defendant is on trial for aggravated battery. Although he was not the initial aggressor, defendant drew a box cutter during a fight and injured two of his opponents. He claims self-defense. Defendant files a motion in limine to exclude evidence that defendant has twice been convicted of the felony of aggravated battery after altercations in which he brandished sharp cutting instruments. Both convictions occurred after the incident for which he is currently on trial. At a hearing on the motion, the following testimony is offered.

The first witness, an assistant district attorney, testified:

Q: Now, did you prosecute the defendant, for an event that occurred on September 12, last year?

A: I did.

Q: And the charge arising from September 12, was an aggravated battery with great bodily harm; is that correct?

A: That's correct.

Q: Was there a weapon used in the case on September 12, of last year?

A: There was.

Q: What type of weapon?

A: The wounds were consistent with a sharp cutting instrument.

The second witness, a police captain, testified:

Q: Calling your attention specifically to December 5, of last year, are you aware of an assault, an aggravated battery-that is, the use of a deadly weapon-that occurred on or about December 5, involving the defendant?

A: Yes, I am familiar with that incident.

Q: And can you tell us, how you were involved in that case?

A: I was a patrol lieutenant at the time, and I was working the evening shift from 4:00 in the afternoon until 2:00 in the morning, and we received a dispatch indicating that a man was injured in an alley.

Q: Had that man been, in fact, assaulted?

A: Yes. He had been stabbed several times.

Q: Can you tell us, was there an investigation made to determine how that stabbing occurred or what instrument was used for that stabbing?

A: Yes, there was an investigation.

Q: Did it in fact lead to the finding of the instrument that was responsible for the stabbing of the victim?

A: Yes. The weapon was located that night.

Q: And what kind of weapon was it?

A: It was a box cutter with a large razor blade.

Q: You are aware, are you not, that defendant pled guilty to that December 5, event; is that correct?

A: Yes, he did.

How should the court rule?

H. Bad Acts

10.25   Refer to problem 10.20. Answer the questions again, this time, however, assume that the witness was arrested for the four criminal acts, but none of the arrests led to a conviction.

10.26   Plaintiff brought suit against a driver of a truck that struck him when he tried to repair his parked motorcycle on shoulder of the freeway. Plaintiff testified that he had income of $75,000 per year and introduced amended tax returns covering the prior three years that declared an income of $75,000. Defendant now seeks to cross-examine the plaintiff concerning the original tax returns for these same three years and to introduce copies of those tax returns. The originally filed tax returns show income of $25,000, $26,000 and $27,000. Defense counsel objects. What result?

10.27 Plaintiff, a school teacher, brought a civil action against a fellow teacher for sexual harassment. Plaintiff's counsel attempts to cross-examine the defendant as follows:

Q: You've been employed by the school district for nine years, correct?

A: Yes.

Q: When you applied for your current job nine years ago you submitted a resume with the application, didn' you?

A: Yes.

Q: Now on that resume you indicated that you had been on the Dean's List in college, correct?

By Defense Counsel: Objection, your honor. This is impermissible impeachment.

By The Court: Overruled. The witness may answer.

A: Yes.

Q: The fact is, however, you were never on the Dean's List were you?

By Defense Counsel: Again, your honor, I object. This is impermissible impeachment

By The Court: Overruled. The witness may answer.

A: No.

Was the court correct in its rulings?

10.28 In a criminal prosecution for conspiracy to distribute cocaine, defendant takes the witness stand and denies involvement in any criminal activity. Eighteen months ago the defendant was arrested for his involvement in a scheme to defraud homeowners. He and a partner, Herbert, were alleged to have tried to sell driveway repaving services, take the money, and then not perform the services. These charges were ultimately dropped when one witness moved out of state and another refused to cooperate with the prosecutor.

.1 On cross-examination of the defendant, the prosecutor asks, "Isn't it true you were arrested last year for attempted fraud?" Defense counsel objected. The judge sustains the objection. Was the court's ruling correct? How might the prosecutor rephrase the question?

.2 Assuming on cross-examination the defendant denies any connection with the fraud scheme, may the prosecutor call Herbert, who will testify to the defendant's involvement in the fraud scheme?

.3 If the judge allowed questioning concerning the driveway scam, could the defendant successfully claim his privilege against self-incrimination concerning the scheme, or has he waived the privilege by taking the witness stand?

10.29   In problem 10.28, assume defendant is charged with intent to defraud, based on a scheme to sell aluminum siding. Would your answer to any of the questions change? If the judge allowed any type of questioning, could the defendant claim his privilege against self-incrimination, or has he waived the privilege by taking the witness stand?

10.30   *Donato v. Donato.* Refer to problem 10.18.2. On cross-examination Vitti is asked:

Q: You know same Gordon, don't you?

A: Yes.

Q: In fact, you met him before Gina and Paul separated, is that right?

A: Yes.

Q: You don't like him do you?

A: Well, I don't know.

Q: You've had disagreements in the past, correct?

A: Yes.

Q: In fact, two years ago you lost your temper?

A: I guess.

Q: You smashed Paul's car windshield, didn't you?

Objection. Improper specific acts.

What is the appropriate ruling on the objection?

10.31   Defendant is alleged to have masterminded a pyramid scheme that stole nearly twenty million dollars from over five hundred people. Defendant seeks to impeach a prosecution witness concerning criminal charges that are currently pending against the witness for indecent assault and battery of a child. The prosecutor objects. What result?

10.32   Defendant is on trial for illegal importation and distribution of drugs. Defendant has been arrested on two prior occasions for drug smuggling. Charges stemming from those two incidents are still pending. On direct examination, defendant testified that he worked with disadvantaged children, and would not have smuggled drugs "for a million dollars." He added that he had never used drugs and would not touch them. In rebuttal, the prosecutor calls a witness who will testify that he was present at the prior two drug transactions and that defendant sold smuggled drugs on those two occasions. Defense counsel objects. What result?

I. Opinion or Reputation

10.33   In a criminal prosecution for tax evasion, the defendant calls as his only witness, Wally, a co-worker for the past three years. Wally will testify to the defendant's lawfulness.

.1 Conduct the examination for defense counsel.

.2 May the prosecutor bring in reputation or opinion evidence of Wally's untruthfulness?

.3 May the prosecutor bring in reputation or opinion evidence of Wally's unlawfulness?

.4 May the prosecutor bring in reputation or opinion evidence of the defendant's untruthfulness?

.5 May the prosecutor bring in reputation or opinion evidence of defendant's unlawfulness?

.6 Conduct the cross-examination of Wally.

J. Rehabilitation

10.34   *Paula v. David and PDG.* In Paula's case-in-chief, Wanda testifies that the light was green for Paula.

.1 David calls Walter who testifies that the light was green for David. May Paula, in rebuttal, call a witness who will testify that in her opinion Wanda is a truthful person?

.2 Wanda is impeached on cross-examination with a prior inconsistent statement in which she told an insurance investigator that the light was green for David. As her second witness, may Paula call a witness who will testify that in her opinion Wanda is truthful?

.3 Wanda is impeached by showing she was the sister of Paula. As a second witness, may Paula call a witness who will testify that in her opinion Wanda is truthful?

K. Constitutional Implications

10.35 *State v. Duffy.* Prior to trial, as the result of a motion Arlo filed, the statement he made to Officer Gorham was suppressed as having been obtained in violation of his *Miranda* rights.

.1 Assume Arlo takes the witness stand and on direct examination he states that he never owned a briefcase. On cross-examination may he be impeached with his statement to Officer Gorham?

.2 Assume Arlo takes the stand, testifies consistently with his statement to Officer Gorham, except he does not mention the briefcase. On cross-examination, the following takes place:

Q: You had a briefcase, didn't you Arlo?

A: No.

Q: In fact, Arlo, you'd admit, wouldn't you, that this briefcase, State's Exhibit 9, at least looks like the one you had, doesn't it?

A: Like I said, I never had a briefcase.

May Arlo now be impeached with his statement to Officer Gorham?

.3 Assume Arlo does not take the witness stand, but he does call Beatrice to testify on his behalf. Bea testifies that in all the years she has known Arlo he has never had a briefcase. May the prosecutor use Arlo's statement to Officer Gorham to attack the credibility of Bea?

10.36 Refer to problem 4.74. Assume the statement to Robert is excluded based on the defendant's Sixth Amendment right to counsel. Defendant takes the stand and denies any involvement in the murders. May the prosecutor call Robert to impeach the defendant's testimony?

Chapter 11

JUDICIAL NOTICE

11.1 Which of the following may be judicially noticed in a federal district court? Would your answer change depending on whether the suit is civil or criminal? Even if admissible in both civil and criminal cases, would the evidence be treated any differently? How would a lawyer request the court to take judicial notice of any of these items?

.1 In the federal district in which you reside, the Richmond Times-Dispatch is a newspaper with a statewide distribution in Virginia.

.2 In the federal district in which you reside, the New York Times is a newspaper with a nationwide distribution.

.3 The 1000 block of E. Main Street in Richmond, Virginia, is in the financial district.

.4 The city of Battle Creek, Michigan, is the world headquarters of the W.K. Kellogg Company.

.5 The W.K. Kellogg Company's headquarters is located on the heart of Battle Creek's downtown.

.6 There were thirteen original colonies.

.7 Electricity is dangerous.

.8 Whiskey causes intoxication.

.9 Intoxication may cause recklessness.

.10 It is impossible to drive from Albany, New York, to New York City in one hour, if you stay within the speed limit. Would it make any difference if the judge had driven from Albany to New York City?

.11 The telephone number of a particular business in New York City.

.12 Cocaine is derived from coca leaves.

.13 Asbestos causes cancer.

.14 The speed of light and sound.

.15 The population of New York City.

.16 Teenagers engage in sexual intercourse and have unwanted pregnancies.

.17 If one spouse is compelled to testify against the other spouse in a criminal action the marital relationship will be destroyed.

.18 If one spouse chooses to testify against the other spouse in a criminal action there is no relationship left to be destroyed.

11.2   Defendant is on trial for being a felon in possession of a firearm. Defendant's predicate felony offense was a 10 year old plea of *nolo contendere* to a charge of possession of a controlled substance. Prior to trial, the government files a motion requesting that the district court take judicial notice of the fact that a violation of this statute is a crime punishable by imprisonment for a term exceeding one year and that under state law a plea of *nolo contendere* is the same as a plea of guilty. Defendant's counsel opposed this motion. How should the court rule?

11.3   Defendant is on trial for conspiracy to commit naturalization and passport fraud. It is alleged that he bribed Charlie, a corrupt government official, to assist him in fraudulently obtaining naturalization and thereafter using the fraudulently obtained naturalization certificate to fraudulently procure his passport. The government asks the trial court to take judicial notice of the guilty plea entered by Charlie to the charges stemming from the same conspiracy. Defense counsel's objects based on the Confrontation Clause. How should the court rule?

11.4   Defendant is on trial in federal court for receipt and possession of images involving the sexual exploitation of minors "shipped or transported in interstate or foreign commerce . . . by any means including by computer." The images were found on defendant's computer hard drive. The computer was connected to the Internet. May the court take judicial notice of the fact that the images moved across state lines?

11.5   Defendant is charged with larceny of goods over $100, a felony. It is alleged he stole a stereo system from the home of Marlene. On direct, the prosecutor has Marlene identify the stereo as the one that was stolen. She then testifies that she bought it in Venezuela two weeks prior to the theft for 6,000 Bolivars. The prosecutor's only other witness is the police officer who testifies to having seized the stereo from the defendant pursuant to a lawful search of the defendant's apartment. The prosecutor then rests. Defendant takes the stand and denies having stolen the stereo. Defendant then rests. The jury returns a verdict of guilty. Defendant then moves for judgment of acquittal based on the prosecutor's failure to establish an essential element, that is, that the value of the goods was in excess of $1,000.

.1 Assume the court grants the motion, and the government appeals. The government asks the appellate court to take judicial notice of the fact that 6,000 Bolivars was more than $1,000 at the exchange rate at the time of Marlene's purchase. What result?

.2 Assume the court denied the motion and the defendant appeals. The defendant asks the appellate court to take judicial notice of the fact that

6,000 Bolivars was less than $1,000 at the exchange rate at the time of Marlene's purchase. What result?

.3 Would it make a difference if the case was tried to a judge as opposed to a jury?

11.6 DRAFTING JURY INSTRUCTIONS. Refer to problem 11.1.10.

.1 Assume this information concerning travel time is offered by the prosecution in a criminal action and the court takes judicial notice. Draft the jury instruction explaining to the jury the use to which it can, or must, place the information.

.2 Assume this information concerning travel time is offered by the defendant in a criminal action and the court takes judicial notice. Draft the jury instruction explaining to the jury the use to which it can, or must, place the information.

.3 Assume this information concerning travel time is offered in a civil action and the court takes judicial notice. Draft the jury instruction explaining to the jury the use to which it can, or must, place the information.

Chapter 12

PRIVILEGES

A. Attorney-Client

12.1 *Paula v. David and PDG.* Paula goes to see Alice Meadows, an attorney. During her meeting with Alice, Paula tells her about the accident. Paula admits that, while she is sure she had the green light, she was going ten miles over the speed limit at the time of the accident.

.1 Assume Paula went to Alice to see if Alice would represent her in a lawsuit against the driver of the truck. Alice explains to Paula that she will need to do some preliminary fact investigation before she can decide whether to take the case. One week later Alice tells Paula that she has decided not to take the case. In the subsequent trial, in which Paula is represented by Brewster Rawls, may defense counsel call Alice as a witness to testify that she was told by Paula that she was speeding at the time of the accident?

.2 Suppose Alice was a long time family friend of Paula's and that Alice was retired. Assume Paula went to Alice, not to see if Alice would represent her, but to seek a recommendation for an attorney who would represent her. Alice recommends Brewster. May defense counsel call Alice as a witness to testify that she was told by Paula that Paula was speeding at the time of the accident?

.3 May Paula be asked on cross-examination, "Were you speeding at the time of the accident?"

12.2 *State v. Duffy.* When Arlo was arrested he was taken to the station house for booking. Arlo refused to talk to the police and demanded a public defender. Arlo was then taken into an interview room and told to sit down. He was also told that a public defender would be in to see him in a few minutes. About five minutes later, Carl walked into the interview room. Arlo, seeing, Carl dressed in a dark suit, exclaimed, "Finally! You got'ta help me mister, they've caught me in the bank job." Carl turns out to be the precinct captain. At trial may Carl testify that Arlo made this statement?

12.3 Criminal investigation for income tax fraud. Arnold is an attorney who specializes in federal income tax.

.1 Carl, a client of Arnold, is under investigation by a grand jury. Arnold's work for Carl has been limited to completing Carl's personal income tax return for the past three years. The grand jury has subpoenaed all records in Arnold's possession that relate to Carl's income tax obligations. Arnold asserts attorney-client privilege. What result?

.2 After years of cheating on her income tax, Angela hires Arnold to send a check to the IRS for back taxes. The theory Alice is working under is that she will pay the back taxes anonymously in the hope that if she is ever caught the penalty she will face will be reduced because she has paid the money. Can a court force Arnold to reveal Angela's identity to the IRS?

12.4 You are an assistant attorney general representing the state in a disability discrimination lawsuit brought by Peter. Peter, who is hearing impaired, brought suit against a local school system, the state Department of Transportation, and the state Department of Education, when he was denied a school bus driver's license. The defendants have just been served with a request to produce documents concerning the Department of Transportation's policy discussions resulting in the promulgation of the regulation that prohibits issuance of a school bus license to anyone who wears a hearing aid. You have two documents in your possession. The first is a cover letter from the Department of Transportation, written in response to your request that they search for documents concerning the denial of drivers licenses. The letter says, in relevant part:

> Enclosed please find the minutes of our January Policy Committee meeting. They don't look very good. As you'll see, Dr. Able, appears to have made the only statement concerning the use of hearing aids and it doesn't look like the Committee seriously questioned the matter.

The second document states:

> The proposed regulation denying school bus licenses to those in need of hearing aids was presented. It was asked whether there was any statistical evidence that there was a greater risk of an accident if the driver needed a hearing aid. Dr. Able responded that he did not know of any, but he did recall once reading a study that hearing impaired drivers in general tend to be more cautious drivers.

Must you turn these two documents over to plaintiff's counsel?

12.5 The parents of a severely disabled student bring suit against a local school system. The parents allege the school system is failing to provide the child with an appropriate education as required by state and federal law.

.1 The parents' counsel seeks to interview the school psychologist to determine the basis for the psychologist's recommendation that the child receive a particular educational placement. The psychologist is a full-time employee of the school system. May the interview take place without the consent of opposing counsel? Would it make a difference if the psychologist were a named defendant?

.2 At trial, the psychologist is called by the school system. On cross-examination, the parents' counsel asks:

Q: Did you have an opportunity to discuss this case with counsel for the school system?

A: Yes.

Q: During that conversation what reservations about the educational program did you tell him you had?

At this point counsel for the school objected. What ruling?

.3 Assume the psychologist is called by the school system. On cross-examination, the psychologist the following occurs:

Q: Did you review any documents prior to coming in to testify today?

A: Yes.

Q: You did that to refresh your memory, correct?

A: Yes.

Q: What documents did you review?

A: All of the educational and medical records submitted to the court.

Q: Anything else?

A: Well, I also reviewed a letter that I sent to the school's attorney where in which I discussed what my likely testimony would be.

Counsel then asks the court to order production of the letter. The school's attorney objects based on attorney-client privilege and attorney work product. How should the court rule?

12.6 Opinion Letter. Refer to problem 4.35. As a result of this and other lawsuits, the hospital in which the events described took place is taking a new look at its risk management procedures. As a result, it wishes to devise an internal investigation procedure that will allow it effectively to investigate alleged actions of malpractice and take corrective actions. The hospital has asked for an opinion letter from you that outlines a procedure that will allow such an investigation to occur, minimize the likelihood that anything uncovered by the hospital would be discoverable in subsequent litigation, and maximize the likelihood that anything favorable will be admissible in subsequent litigation.

12.7 In problem 12.1.1, suppose that instead of talking to Alice, Paula's meeting was with a paralegal in Alice's office. Could the paralegal be required to relate the statement?

12.8 *Paula v. David and PDG.* Brewster sent Paula to an economist for the purpose of questioning her so that the economist could testify at trial as to the extent of Paula's lost lifetime income. At trial, can Paula be asked on cross-examination what she told the economist during that interview?

12.9 *Donato v. Donato.* Assume Paul made the additional allegation that Gina abuses the children on a regular basis. During the course of his investigation, Gina's attorney becomes convinced that Paul's allegations are true. The attorney confronts Gina with the evidence, and she admits she abuses the children. What action if any should Gina's lawyer take under the following circumstances?

    .1 On cross-examination by Paul's lawyer, Gina denies abusive behavior?

    .2 The state has a statute which requires "professionals" to report child abuse to Child and Protective Services.

12.10 Federal law requires reporting to the IRS cash transactions in excess of $10,000. Defendant is charged with failure to report $10,000 cash transactions to the IRS. The prosecution asserts that the defendant, an attorney, was laundering drug money by depositing the drug money into his business account. Specifically, the defendant took $100,000 and made 12 separate deposits each totaling less than the $10,000. Defendant was arrested after the manager of defendant's bank reported the transactions to the IRS and the FBI. The prosecutor seeks to call defendant's lawyer and ask whether it is true that the defendant had previously come to the lawyer and asked if a cash transaction involving the $100,000 could avoid being reported by the bank, if indeed, he broke up the deposits so that each totaled less than $10,000. Defendant objects based on the attorney-client privilege. What ruling? How can the judge rule on the objection without breaching the privilege?

12.11 *Paula v. David and PDG.* Refer to problem 3.8. During his deposition, Walter was asked how he prepared for his deposition. Walter indicated that he had spoken to Paula and she had given him her notes. Defense counsel files a pre-trial motion seeking discovery of the notes. What result?

12.12 OFFICE PROCEDURE/DRAFTING. Draft the cover sheet for your law office fax transmissions. What issues need to be addressed in drafting this form?

B. Physician-Patient/Psychotherapist-Patient

12.13 In which of the following circumstances could the patient, or a representative of the patient, successfully assert a privilege?

.1 *Paula v. David and PDG.* David seeks to introduce the testimony of Paula's physician concerning the physical condition of Paula prior to the accident.

.2 *Paula v. David and PDG.* David seeks to introduce the testimony of the physician to whom Brewster sent Paula for the purpose of allowing the physician to prepare to testify at trial.

.3 *Paula v. David and PDG.* David seeks to call and question the physician that treated Paula at the emergency room immediately following the accident. Would it affect your answer if the physician were questioned only about what he saw, not what Paula told him?

.4 *Donato v. Donato.* Gina seeks to have the psychiatrist who has been treating Paul testify concerning the psychotherapy that Paul has been receiving for the past three years. Suppose the witness was a psychologist, or a psychiatric social worker, would that affect your answer?

.5 *State v. Duffy.* The prosecutor seeks to call Arlo's family physician who will testify that the day after the robbery Arlo came to him for treatment of a skin rash, apparently caused by a red dye covering his hands.

.6 *Donato v. Donato.* Assume that Paul and Gina had a fourth child, Harold, who committed suicide two years ago. Gina seeks to call the psychologist who had been treating Harold at the time of Harold's death.

12.14 Plaintiff, a health insurance company, brings a civil suit in federal court seeking damages from defendant, a medical laboratory. Plaintiff alleges defendant engaged in fraudulent testing procedures and false diagnoses of plaintiff's insureds amounting to violation of the federal Racketeer Influenced and Corrupt Organization Act. Plaintiff seeks discovery from defendant of records of specific patients plaintiff insured and who had lab tests conducted by defendant. Defendant objects citing the physician-patient privilege. What result?

12.15 Defendant is on trial in federal court for the murder of an FBI agent. On direct examination defendant testified that his mental status, specifically dementia caused by a sexually transmitted disease, made him incapable of forming the required intent to commit the crime. In rebuttal, the prosecutor seeks to introduce the following records. Defendant objects based on privilege. How should the court rule?

.1 Medical records of a physician who treated defendant for the disease before the killing.

.2 Records of psychiatrist and a psychologist, both of whom treated defendant before the killing.

.3 Records of a clinical social worker who treated the defendant before the killing.

C. Spousal Privileges

12.16   Defendant, Danny, is charged with conspiracy to distribute cocaine. On the day of arrest, Danny told his wife, Sarah, "We better break out the savings, I finally got caught."

.1 May Sarah be called by the prosecutor to testify that Danny made this statement?

.2 Suppose Sarah chose to testify, would your answer change?

.3 Suppose Danny and Sarah got divorced between Danny's arrest and his trial. Would the divorce affect your answer?

.4 While out on bail, Danny has Sarah drive him to his lawyer's office to prepare for trial. Sarah joins Danny in the attorney's office, where the defendant admits that he was involved in a plan to sell cocaine. At trial can the wife be asked about this admission? Could the lawyer be asked?

12.17   In a civil action brought by a corporation, a former employee is sued to recover improper expenditures using a company credit card. The plaintiff calls the wife of the defendant and asks, "After your husband left the company, did he continue to use the company credit card?" Defendant objects. What result?

Chapter 13

BURDENS OF PROOF AND PRESUMPTIONS

A. Burdens of Proof

13.1 *Paula v. David and PDG.* The lawsuit is brought in federal court, based on diversity of citizenship jurisdiction. State law requires that in any personal injury action the party alleging injury shall have "the burden of proof on the issue of that person's lack of contributory negligence." Federal Rule of Civil Procedure 8 requires contributory negligence to be pleaded as an affirmative defense by the defendant. In light of the *Erie* doctrine, can the state law and federal rule be reconciled?

B. Civil Presumptions

13.2 *Donato v. Donato.* Assume that Gina's mother has changed her mind and now believes Gina's relationship with Sam Gordon is harmful to the children. Her mother, however, also believes that Paul is not a proper person to have custody of the children. She, therefore, is seeking custody. Additional legal research reveals a controlling state supreme court case that provides:

> In a custody dispute between a parent and a non parent, the law presumes that the child's best interests will be served when in the custody of its parent.

Another controlling state supreme court case states:

> Although the presumption favoring a parent over a non parent is a strong one, it is rebutted when certain factors are established by clear and convincing evidence. We have held such factors include: (1) parental unfitness, (2) a previous order of divestiture, (3) voluntary relinquishment, and (4) abandonment. Finally, we have recognized a fifth factor that rebuts this presumption: a finding of special facts and circumstances constituting an extraordinary reason for taking the child from its parent or parents.

Discuss the meaning and impact of the presumptions in what is now a three-way custody dispute.

13.3 In a medical malpractice action brought in federal court based on diversity. Plaintiff is called as the first witness. The first question plaintiff's counsel asks is does he know how much he has incurred in medical expenses from the date of his injury to the date he compiled his medical bills before the commencement of the trial.

State law provides:

§ 41. Proof that medical, hospital, and doctor bills were paid or incurred because of any illness, disease, or injury shall be prima facie evidence that such bills so paid or incurred were necessary and reasonable.

.1 Defense counsel objects. What result?

.2 Assume the state's supreme court has interpreted the statute as simplifying the procedure for proving medical expenses as an element of a claim by (1) permitting a claimant, based on his or her testimony, to identify and introduce medical bills incurred because of the illness, disease, or injury sued upon; and (2) establishing the bills so identified and introduced as prima facie evidence and a rebuttable presumption that the expenses were necessary and reasonable. What result?

C. Criminal Presumptions

13.4   Assume you are a staff attorney with a state legislature's Legislative Services Office. The legislature is in session and you have been asked to provide an opinion on the following proposed changes to the state's criminal code. Your opinion is sought both as to the legal basis for these bills, as well as the practical consequence if these bills become law.

.1 A senator from a rural district is concerned with a growing problem: people dumping trash on farm land and in forests. When the senator approached the local prosecutors, each indicated that it was difficult to obtain a conviction, because it is difficult to connect the suspect to the particular trash. The senator, therefore, wishes to introduce a bill that would provide:

Any trash, litter, refuse or other discarded material found in violation of the state's litter laws and that has material containing the name or address of any person shall be presumed to have been deposited in that place by the person so indicated or the person or persons living at the address indicated therein.

Does it matter whether the litter laws involve civil or criminal penalties?

.2 Concerned with the rise in thefts in his city, and the apparent free flow of stolen goods on the street, another senator wishes to introduce a bill that would provide:

Any person purchasing any goods at less than 50 percent of the goods fair market value shall be presumed to have known the goods were stolen.

13.5 *State v. Duffy.* The second armed robbery charge on Arlo's Record of Arrest involves a robbery of a luggage store. Assume that during a proper search of Arlo's apartment, additional briefcases and pieces of luggage were found, all identified as having been taken from the luggage store that was robbed. Arlo is now on trial for armed robbery of the luggage store. The following quotations from two state supreme court cases are controlling:

> It is a general rule of the common law that the possession of goods recently stolen is *prima facie* evidence of guilt, and the burden of accounting for that possession is thrown upon the accused.

> The unexplained possession of recently stolen goods raises an inference that the possessor is the thief.

Are these statements consistent? Discuss the meaning and impact of these two cases in relation to Arlo's trial of armed robbery of the luggage store.

13.6 *Paula v. David and PDG.* Assume David was given a blood alcohol test immediately after the accident. The results of the test showed a blood alcohol content of.11. David is charged with driving a vehicle while intoxicated. State law provides:

> § 18.2-269 In any prosecution for driving a vehicle while intoxicated the amount of alcohol in the blood of the accused as indicated by chemical analysis shall give rise to the following presumptions:

> (1) If there was 0.05 percent or less it shall be presumed that the accused was not under the influence of alcoholic intoxicants;

> (2) If there was in excess of 0.05 percent, but less than 0.10 percent, such facts shall not give rise to any presumption;

> (3) If there was 0.10 percent or more it shall be presumed that the accused was under the influence of alcoholic intoxicants.

Discuss the impact and meaning of this statutory provision in David's criminal trial. Assume the statute was specifically not limited to criminal prosecutions. Would the impact be any different in the civil action? Despite its specific reference to criminal actions, in the subsequent civil action, will the statutory provision play any role?

13.7 Defendants are on trial for selling marijuana to undercover police officers. The state penal code provides:

> § 18.2-248. **Penalties for manufacture, sale, gift, distribution or possession of a controlled drug.** — It shall be unlawful for any person to manufacture, sell, give, distribute or possess with intent to manufacture, sell, give or distribute a controlled substance.

> (a) Any person who violates this section with respect to a controlled substance classified in Schedules I, II or III shall upon conviction be imprisoned for not less than five nor more than forty years and fined not

more than twenty-five thousand dollars; and provided further that if such person prove that he gave, distributed or possessed with intent to give or distribute marijuana or a controlled substance classified in Schedule III only as an accommodation to another individual and not with intent to profit thereby nor to induce the recipient or intended recipient of the controlled substance to use or become addicted to or dependent upon such controlled substance, he shall be guilty of a Class 1 misdemeanor.

§ 18.2-263. **Unnecessary to negative exception, etc.; burden of proof of exception, etc.** — In any complaint, information, or indictment, and in any action or proceeding brought for the enforcement of any provision of this article or of The Drug Control Act §§ 54-524.1 et seq.), it shall not be necessary to negative any exception, excuse, proviso, or exemption contained in this article or in The Drug Control Act, and the burden of proof of any such exception, excuse, proviso, or exemption shall be upon the defendant.

Defendants contend that the sale of marijuana was an accommodation. He further contends that sale as an accommodation is a lesser included offense of a sale of marijuana for profit. What is the practical impact of the success or failure of defendant's argument that sale as an accommodation is a lesser included offense?

Chapter 14

ASSESSMENT, INTEGRATION & REVIEW

14.1 Refer to problem 9.29. The prosecutor seeks to introduce a safety deposit box key registered to the defendant that was found in the search of the bedroom. Defendant objects. What ruling?

14.2 Defendant is on trial for murder. Defendant calls to the stand a police officer. During direct examination, the defendant seeks to introduce handwritten notes made by the police officer. The notes summarize the content of anonymous phone calls received from individuals who called the police department with tips related to the criminal investigation of the murder. According to the handwritten notes, some of the tipsters indicated that a specifically named individual other than the defendant committed the crime. Other tipsters simply stated that the defendant did not commit the crime. The prosecution objects to the introduction of the notes, arguing that they are irrelevant and hearsay. How should the court rule?

14.3 On direct examination the witness is asked to describe the type of car he saw driving away from the scene of a drive-by shooting. The witness says that he is having a hard time remembering. Counsel asks, "Was it a domestic car?" Defense counsel objects. What ruling?

14.4 Defendant was arrested for driving under the influence of alcohol. The arresting police officer immediately took the defendant to the police station where a town judge questioned the defendant and found probable cause to arrest and hold him. At the subsequent felony trial before a different judge, the prosecutor seeks to call the judge at the police station to testify that the defendant was drunk on the night in question. Defense counsel objects. How should the court rule?

14.5 Is the following evidence hearsay? If it is hearsay, is it admissible anyway? Unless the declarant is identified as P (plaintiff/prosecutor) or D (defendant), assume he or she is not a party.

.1 To prove that X has heard of Albany Law School, testimony by Y that X said, "I intend to enroll in the Albany Law School next fall."

.2 To prove that X was a student at the Albany Law School in September, 2009, P calls a neighbor of X who will testify that he saw a letter addressed to X on Albany Law School letterhead that said, "We are happy to inform you that you have been accepted into the entering class beginning in August, 2009."

.3 Same issue as previous problem. The witness attempts to testify that on April 30, 2009, X said, "I'm going to Albany Law School in the fall."

.4 Same issue as previous problem. The witness attempts to testify that on May 1, 2009, X said, "I was accepted at Albany Law School yesterday."

.5 To prove that X was not a student at Albany Law School, X's mother's testimony that she made an inquiry and received a letter from the University registrar that said X was not a student.

.6 To prove T lacked the ability to make a will, testimony of Y that on several occasions, T said, "I'm Bill Clinton."

.7 In criminal action, to prove that the assailant was D, testimony by a police officer that while viewing a line-up, the victim pointed to D and began to cry.

.8 To prove that D had a motive to rob a bank, testimony by X that he heard Y say to D, "I need the money, or there will be serious consequences."

.9 To establish the identity of the bank robber, the prosecution offers a videotape of the robbery taken by a bank camera.

.10 To prove that D committed armed robbery, X, a police officer, will testify that two days after the robbery, he interviewed a bystander who said that he saw D run out of the bank.

.11 To prove that D committed armed robbery, X, a police officer, seeks to read from notes that he took while interviewing a bystander who said that he saw D run out of the bank.

.12 In a negligence action, P, a carnival patron, is injured on a ride when the floor collapses. W testifies that just before the accident, X, a ride operator, told D, the ride owner, "Your floor boards are rotted and will break soon."

.13 In the previous problem, X testifies that just before the accident, he told D, "Your floor boards are rotted and are close to breaking."

.14 To prove the time of day that an accident occurred, X will testify that she knew it was 10:00 a.m., because she had just looked at her watch.

.15 Two defendants, D1 and D2, are on trial for conspiracy to commit armed robbery of a liquor store and with the actual armed robbery. X, a police officer, will testify that after D1 was arrested, D1 said that D2 told him that he (D2) had committed the robbery. Neither D1 nor D2 will testify.

.16 P v. D. To prove that A was an agent of D, P offers testimony of W that A said, "I am an agent of D."

.17 To prove that D murdered the night manager of the Lakeside Bowling Alley, the prosecution seeks to introduce testimony by a police officer that at the time of his arrest, D had in his possession a score card printed with the logo from the Lakeside Bowling Alley.

.18 On the issue of whether a P had an infection, D calls a nurse, N, who will testify that the doctor gave antibiotics to P.

.19 Same issue as previous problem. N seeks to testify that she heard the doctor, M, say to P, "I'm sorry to tell you the test results were positive, indicating there was an infection."

.20 Same issue as previous problem. The doctor, M, seeks to testify, "After reviewing the results of the lab report and after hearing from Dr. Smith about his conclusion that P had an infection, I arrived at the same conclusion."

.21 Negligence action arising from car/truck collision. To establish that P suffered damages in the accident, P testifies that as he lay pinned under his car, he told a rescue worker, "Please help, my leg hurts."

.22 Same case as previous problem. X testifies that as he began to treat Y, a passenger in the car, Y said, "No, go help P; the truck hit his side of the car."

.23–.25 Albany Law School is the only named defendant in a lawsuit. The Law School is being sued under federal law for failure to provide a reasonable accommodation to a student with a disability. Plaintiff alleges she has a learning disability and requires double time on exams. The Associate Dean refused to allow the exam accommodation.

> **.23** Plaintiff seeks to testify that the Associate Dean of the Law School said to the plaintiff, "I'm sorry, if it were up to me, I would provide the accommodation. Unfortunately, it's up to the Vice President for Student Affairs."

> **.24** When plaintiff originally sought the accommodation, the Associate Dean requested documentation of the disability from a qualified expert. Plaintiff had her educational diagnostician (an appropriate expert) write a letter to the Associate Dean that said, "Plaintiff requires extra time on exams as a result of a learning disability." Plaintiff, while she is on the stand, seeks to introduce this letter from her educational diagnostician.

> **.25** Plaintiff calls Wanda, a fellow law student who, if allowed, will testify that during the evidence midterm, she heard Plaintiff say to herself, "It just takes me so long to read this."

.26–.33 Defendant is charged with the drive by shooting of Victor. It is alleged that defendant and Victor were members of rival gangs. The prosecutor alleges that Victor and the defendant were personal enemies as the result of an altercation that occurred at Monroe High School between gang members. As a result of the altercation, a member of the defendant's gang was killed. It is alleged that Danny participated in the killing. Danny himself was recently killed in a liquor store robbery.

.26 The prosecutor calls Walter. Walter is presently in the county jail serving a two-month sentence for shoplifting. Walter will testify, if allowed, that his cell mate, Danny told him (Walter) that he (Danny) and defendant, "off'ed Victor in retaliation for Victor having killed a mutual friend." Danny himself was recently killed in a liquor store robbery.

.27 Assume Danny is alive. If allowed, Danny will testify that as defendant pulled the trigger, Danny said, "That's for Mark."

.28 The defendant calls to the stand a witness who will testify that defendant's reputation in the community in which he lives is that he is nonviolent.

.29 To prove that defendant was not in town on the day of the shooting (August 24), defendant calls a neighbor of defendant who will testify that he saw a letter addressed to defendant on Boy Scouts of America letterhead. Part of the letter said, "The International Travel Committee is pleased to announce that your application to travel to Germany August 23–27 has been accepted."

.30 At the time of the shooting, Defendant worked part-time in a grocery store. To prove Defendant was not in town on the day in question, defense counsel calls the grocery store owner, who will bring with him time sheets that show that Defendant did not work on the day of the shooting.

.31 To establish that Victor was a student at Monroe High School, the prosecutor calls a police officer to the stand to introduce a document that is purportedly Victor's report card from Monroe High School. The report card was found on Victor's body.

.32 Wanda will, if allowed, testify that two days after the shooting she went to the police and told the police that she saw defendant pull the trigger.

.33 The prosecutor calls a police officer to the stand to introduce a letter purportedly signed by Harold Johnson that states that the writer was standing at his window when he saw the defendant shoot Victor. Assume the letter is authenticated.

.34–.36 Refer to problem 5.8. Perry, dissatisfied with the treatment he received from Dr. Duke, and in great pain, went to a second physician, Dr. Williams. On the issue of whether Perry had an infection:

.34 Dr. Williams offers to testify that when he examined him, Mr. Perry had inflammation, tenderness and a temperature; all symptoms of an infection.

.35 Perry's mother offers to testify that she told the doctor that plaintiff said, "I my leg feels tender and it's swollen, we better go to a doctor."

.36 Perry offers to testify, "My knee was very tender."

.37 To prove the value of a company's stock on a particular day, the *Wall Street Journal* stock market listings for that day.

.38 *State v. Duffy.* To prove Duffy was the bank robber, the prosecution offers evidence that the FBI listed Duffy on its "Ten Most Wanted" list.

.39 P, a law school dean, sues D for defamation. W, a witness for P testifies that D, in front of P and three trustees of the university, said, "You realize, don't you, P has been convicted of income tax evasion?" In defense, D calls a witness who says that what D said was, "You realize, don't you, we are lucky that P hasn't been convicted of income tax evasion like the dean over at State U."

.40 *Paula v. David and PDG.* Walter is called as a witness. Walter remembers the main facts of the accident, but is unclear about some of the details, and needs to have his memory refreshed. Plaintiff's attorney seeks to allow Walter to review a diary entry before continuing his testimony. The diary entry was written by Walter one hour after the intersection collision.

.41 Assume the same situation as in the previous question, except that Walter draws a complete blank about what happened at the time of the accident. He says he recalled it vividly at the time he wrote the diary entry. Plaintiff's attorney wants to have him read the diary entry into evidence.

.42 To prove that defendant is the father of her child, the mother offers a letter from defendant's attorney in which the attorney states that his client has admitted he is the father of the child.

.43 *Paula v. David and PDG.* Wanda testifies that Paula had the green light. On cross-examination, defense counsel offers a portion of the transcript of Wanda's deposition in which Wanda stated that David had the green light.

.44 Criminal prosecution for the theft of stereo systems from a department store warehouse. To prove the value of the stereos, the prosecutor offers a copy of the manufacturer's catalog.

.45 Keith is on trial for possession of cocaine with intent to distribute. A police officer testifies that as he was conducting a legal search of the defendant's apartment, the telephone rang. The police offer picked up the phone and the caller said: "Can I speak to Keith? Does he still have any stuff?"

.46 Prosecution for drug trafficking. Police arrested defendant and seized a pager. The pager while in the possession of the police officer flashed the message, "Did you get the stuff?"

.47 Bank fraud. One of defendants sought to introduce his letter of resignation to the bank. The letter stated he was resigning because he disagreed with the policies and practices of the other defendants, believing them to be illegal.

.48 After viewing defendant the day of the crime, Renzy made a positive identification of defendant the next day. At the trial, held nine months later, however, Renzy made an equivocal in-court identification and testified that the man who ran by her, carrying the purse, "looked like him [pointing to the defendant]." The prosecutor then calls Officer Gaither to testify as to the out-of-court identification made by the witness, Renzy, when Gaither interviewed her the day following the commission of the crime.

.49 Refer to problem 6.5. Paul cannot identify the caller, but he does have "caller ID" on his telephone. This device flashes the telephone number of people who call. Paul's attorney seeks to have Paul testify to the number on the caller ID and then to have the court take judicial notice that the telephone number is listed to Sam.

.50 Age and sex discrimination lawsuit. Plaintiff was not recalled from a layoff and seeks to testify that the employer's son told her that the employer was not going to hire her back because of her age and that the men at work did not like having women around.

14.6   Refer to the previous problem. For each indicate whether the evidence is

A. Admissible as an exception to the hearsay rule.

B. Admissible non hearsay.

C. Inadmissible, hearsay.

D. Inadmissible, because it is irrelevant.

14.7   Refer to problems 14.5.23–14.5.25. The Law School calls a psychologist to testify that in his opinion, the plaintiff did not require the accommodation that was sought. Plaintiff objects. What result?

14.8   Defendant, a well-known sports personality, is on trial for murder. When the police came to arrest him, he tried to escape. His escape attempt was broadcast and simultaneously videotaped by a local television station. The camera team was located in a helicopter. The prosecution calls the television station employee who did the actual videotaping and asks the employee to describe what he saw on the day of the attempted escape. Defense counsel objects. What ruling?

14.9   Murder Prosecution. The prosecutor seeks to introduce a weapon found two blocks from the scene of the crime. The officer who found the weapon will testify that he was doing a routine search following the killing when he picked up the gun. He knows that it is the same gun he seized because he scratched his initials on the handle. Defendant objects. What ruling?

14.10   Defendant is on trial for social security fraud. The government alleges the defendant's mother was paying the daughter to work in the mother's hair salon and the defendant did not report the income. The prosecutor seeks to introduce testimony of a federal agent who will testify that during his investigation of the fraud, defendant's mother told him that entries in the mother's At-A-Glance book represented money she had given to defendant to buy family groceries. The At-A-Glance book was used by the mother to record hair salon appointments in connection with her operation of a beauty salon as well as to make personal notations. Defense counsel objects arguing the testimony is inadmissible hearsay. The mother will not testify, claiming her right against self incrimination.

.1 The first government argument is that the testimony is not offered for the truth of the matter asserted, but offered as a "false exculpatory statement." How should the court rule? Would additional information be useful? If so what information?

.2 The government also argues that the mother's statement and the At-A-Glance book were statements of a coconspirator. How should the court rule? Would additional information be useful? If so what information?

.3 The government argues that the At-A-Glance book is admissible under the business records hearsay exception. How should the court rule?

.4 Assuming the court rules the evidence is either not hearsay or an exception to the hearsay rule what should be defendant's argument be to exclude the evidence anyway?

14.11   Refer to problem 9.4. Plaintiff seeks to introduce evidence that six months after his accident the manufacturer issued a nation-wide recall of the snow blowing machine. The manufacturer objects. What result?

14.12   Joey Alexander is charged with unlawful possession of a firearm by a felon. It is alleged that Alexander telephoned his estranged girlfriend, Yvette Young, at her place of employment and said among other things that he would "do something" to Young and that he would go to her apartment and "mess it" up. Fifteen minutes after receiving the phone call, Young called 911 and related Alexander's statements. Young also stated, "he also has a gun." The dispatcher then asked, "does he have a gun now?" Young replied, "Yeah."

In the fifteen minutes between receiving the call from Alexander and placing the call to 911, Young called her mother to warn her not to go to Young's apartment for fear that Alexander would be there.

A police officer went to Young's place of work 12 minutes after the 911 call as placed. The officer interviewed Young and in response to a question Young stated, "I haven't seen him with a gun today, but he keeps a revolver with a brown handle in his night stand."

Ten minutes after the police officer began to question Young at her work. Alexander showed up during the questioning and threatened to harm Young. The police officer arrested Alexander. In a subsequent search of Alexander's car the police officer discovered a brown handled revolver.

1. The prosecutor seeks to introduce the 911 tape. Defense counsel objects based on hearsay. How should the court rule?

.2 The prosecutor calls the police offer to the stand and seeks to have her testify about what Young told the police officer while interviewing Young at her place of employment. Defense counsel objects based on hearsay. On *voir dire examination*, the police officer testifies that when she first saw Young, Young appeared "stressed, afraid, and frightened." How should the court rule on defense counsel's objection?

.3 Assume that defense counsel also objects to the introduction of the 911 tape arguing that the tape is inadmissible character evidence. How should the court rule?

.4 What other objections should the prosecutor be prepared to overcome in her attempt to introduce the 911 tape?

14.13   To prove that a nonparty corporation had a fax machine, a plaintiff will testify that she received a fax transmission with the corporate logo on it. Defendant objects. What ruling?

14.14   NEGOTIATION OR MOTION IN LIMINE. *State v. Duffy.*
The police have just informed the court that the May 25, letter, envelope and attached bill are lost. The police have no idea where the documents could have gone. The police have searched all known places where the evidence could have been. Preliminary negotiations took place between the prosecutor and defense counsel before it was known that the evidence was lost. The prosecutor had refused to reduce the charge to simple robbery under § 18.2-57, but did agree to recommend a minimum sentence. Arlo was considering whether to accept the offer when defense counsel was informed the documents were missing. Your instructor will assign you *one* of the following tasks. **Be sure to fill out and return the joint questionnaire after completing the session.**

.1 **Negotiation.** Defense counsel has contacted the prosecutor to continue plea discussions. Meet to continue plea discussions. Your instructor will provide you with confidential information concerning your position in this negotiation.

.2 **Negotiation.** The court has informed counsel that counsel should meet to discuss this development. The court would like counsel, if possible, to arrive at an agreement as to the admissibility of testimony concerning the lost items.

.3 **Motion in Limine.**

.1 As defense counsel make a motion in limine on the evidentiary issues raised by this latest development.

.2 As the prosecutor respond to defense counsel's motion.

14.15 Is the summary report in problem 7.11 admissible as an official document?

14.16 Danny U. Fielding is on trial for grand larceny. Danny is charged with using a scheme, along with an accomplice Harold, in which he called Computer Machines International, Inc., (CMI), a large computer manufacturer, and pretended to represent Office Systems Incorporated (OSI), a regular customer of CMI. Using forged documentation, it is alleged that Danny placed an order for computer equipment worth $100,000 and arranged for shipment to OSI, delivery to be made on a specific date. On the delivery date, it is charged, Danny telephoned the OSI warehouse claiming to be from CMI. He told the OSI manager that a mistake had been made and that computer equipment had been improperly shipped to OSI. The prosecutor then claims Danny made arrangements to pick up the computer equipment, this time using forged documentation indicating he was a representative of CMI. The warehouse manager freely gave the equipment to Danny, knowing that he had no record of any such purchase by OSI. Harold has subsequently died in a liquor store robbery.

.1 The prosecutor calls the police officer who investigated the crime and who testifies that he found the stolen computer equipment in a warehouse. Along with the equipment he found shirts bearing a laundry mark 'DUF'. Was this testimony properly admitted?

.2 The police officer also testifies from his notes as to the serial number on each piece of equipment. Is this testimony properly admitted?

.3 The prosecution then calls Walter who testifies that, "I spoke to Harold a couple of days before the crime was supposed to have been committed and he said he was going to get a some new computer equipment. Then a couple weeks later Harold told me, 'I took that equipment from CMI. Of course, Danny helped and now owns half, I guess.'" The prosecution then rested. Is this testimony properly admitted?

.4 Danny testifies in his own behalf that "I have never stolen anything in my life." The prosecution, on cross-examination of Danny, seeks to introduce evidence of Danny's past behavior. Under what circumstances, if any, can the following information be introduced?

A. In Yr-4, Danny confessed to car theft. Danny confessed that he had used forged documents to obtain possession of the car. The confession, however, was inadmissible in a prosecution for that theft because he was not given a *Miranda* warning. Danny was acquitted of that charge.

B. In Yr-12, Danny was convicted of obtaining property under false pretenses. He was sentenced to five years in jail and served three years.

14.17   Defendant is charged with murder. Defendant is alleged to be a member of a street gang called the Bloods. The Government alleges that the murder that occurred was in part the result of the victim failing to show proper respect to members of the gang. The Government seeks to admit the following evidence. Defense counsel objects. What result?

.1 Defendant was a member of the Bloods street gang.

.2 Defendant was previously incarcerated on several occasions for possession of marijuana with intent to distribute.

.3 Defendant was arrested last year for driving while impaired as a result of his marijuana use (a misdemeanor), which led to a search of his vehicle that uncovered a concealed gun (a felony). Charges are still pending on these matters.

.4 On one occasion, Defendant assaulted and shot at two unidentified individuals. The defendant was never charged with the assault.

14.18   COUNSELING. *State v. Duffy.* You represent Arlo Duffy. You are preparing for trial and must decide whether to place Arlo on the witness stand. Counsel Arlo on whether to take the stand in his own defense. Specifically, you should:

1. Obtain any additional information that would affect the decision on whether Arlo should take the stand;

2. Identify the alternatives Arlo has on the issue of whether to take the stand;

3. Discuss the consequences of each of these alternatives, including legal as well as nonlegal consequences and positive was well as negative consequences; and

4. Provide whatever guidance and insight needed in making the decision.

Your instructor will provide the student playing Arlo with confidential information. **Be sure to fill out and return the joint questionnaire after completing the counseling session.**

14.19   WITNESS INTERVIEW. Assume the same facts as in 14.18, including any information gained during that exercise. (Your instructor will provide this information if you have not done 14.18). Arlo has suggested Beatrice Duke as a character witness on his behalf. You have arranged a meeting to interview her to decide whether to call her to testify to the good character of Arlo. Beatrice has been Arlo's on-and-off lover for the past four years. Two years ago they lived together. While they no longer live together, Beatrice does work at the same fast food restaurant as Arlo. Beatrice began work at the restaurant 18 months ago. Arlo has been working there for two and one-half years. Arlo has been pressing you to call Bea as a character witness in his defense. Your instructor will provide the student playing Bea with confidential information. **Be sure to fill out and return the joint questionnaire after completing the interview session.**

14.20 Defendant is charged with illegal possession of cocaine with the intent to distribute. Defendant's partner, Harold, previously pled guilty, and has been sentenced. The prosecutor seeks to introduce videotapes of meetings at which Harold purchased cocaine. Defendant objects. What ruling?

14.21 The City of Chicago enacted an ordinance that restricts the sale of spray paint. By limiting access to spray paint, the City hopes to decrease the amount of graffiti on public and private property. A group of hardware store owners bring suit challenging the constitutionality of the ordinance. Substantive law requires that the court determine the ordinance's impact on interstate commerce. At trial, there is an attempt to introduce the following testimony. Assuming timely objection, how should the court rule?

.1 The city seeks to introduce photographs of painted graffiti.

.2 Expert testimony is offered to establish the economic impact of the ordinance.

.3 Both sides offer expert testimony on the likely deterrent effect of the ordinance.

.4 Plaintiffs seek to testify concerning their belief that the ordinance will have no deterrent effect.

14.22 Defendant is on trial for tax evasion and failure to file income tax returns. Defendant claims he did not intentionally break the law because he did not realize his wages were taxable. At trial, there is an attempt to introduce the following testimony. Assuming timely objection, how should the court rule?

.1 The prosecutor seeks to introduce evidence that five years ago defendant signed settlement documents arising out of a prior dispute with the IRS. The settlement includes a statement in which the defendant forgoes a contention that his wages were not taxable.

.2 The defendant offers testimony by psychiatric expert that defendant is "credible, sincere and manifests a good faith belief" with respect to Internal Revenue Code obligations.

14.23 Plaintiff brings a civil rights action against the city and its police department. She alleges that the police conducted an illegal search of her home. Defendants file a motion in limine with respect to a press release issued by the city. The press release summarizes the results of the city's investigation of the incident giving rise to the lawsuit. The release states that the officers involved exercised poor judgment in failing to read the search warrant thoroughly, and that appropriate disciplinary action would be taken. How should the court rule on the motion to exclude this press release?

14.24   *Paula v. David and PDG.* Paula and David have attended each day of the trial. PDG, however, never sent a representative other than its trial lawyer.

Brewster becomes ill just before closing argument, requiring his associate to conduct the closing. During closing argument, Brewster's associate states the following:

> Don't waste a lot of sympathy thinking that I am going to be pursuing David after this trial, because you can't get blood out of a stone. I hope you give me credit with more intelligence than to pursue somebody out of whom I can obtain no damages. . . .

> . . . .

> Now, defendant's attorney has a high tolerance for pain as a result of representing people such as defendants in this case. . . . I do want to note something, and it is very important. PDG didn't care enough about this case to have anyone present.

Assuming timely objection to the above argument, how should the court rule?

14.25   Defendant is charged with attempting to transport $186,000 out of the country with knowledge that the funds were proceeds from the illegal sale of cocaine. Tests of the seized cash showed that all of the bills were tainted with cocaine. Defendant asks the court to take judicial notice of the fact that a large percentage of United States paper money is tainted with illegal narcotics. The defendant does not direct the court to any particular study. The prosecutor objects. What ruling?

14.26   Complete the Performance Test *In re Berger* in Appendix D.

14.27   Complete the Performance Test *Dodson v. Canadian Equipment Company* in Appendix E.

APPENDIX A

State v. Duffy

POLICE OFFICERS OFFENSE REPORT
CALHOUN POLICE DEPARTMENT

Offense: Armed Robbery
Complainant: First Investors
Address: 249 Main Street   **Phone:** 555-3476
Type of Premises: Bank   **Reported By:** C. Dodge
Date Occurred: 6/1/Yr-0   **Time Occurred:** 1:30
     p.m.

PROPERTY
$3250

Lost [ ] Found [ ] Stolen [ ] Evidence [X]

DETAILS OF OFFENSE

Reporting officer received call that bank robbery was in progress at First Investors Savings Bank, Main St. Proceeded to destination. Arrived at approximately 1:40 p.m.

Upon arrival talked to manager, Cynthia Dodge, who explained perpetrator entered bank at approximately 1:30 p.m. armed with large revolver. Perpetrator ordered the two tellers to place money into a leather brief case. As he left the bank, a small explosive device went off inside the brief case, staining the money. After the device exploded, the robber abandoned the brief case and fled.

Inspection of the brief case which I recovered from a passerby, Roy Smith, who had retrieved it, revealed, concealed in a flap, two envelopes addressed to Arlo P. Duffy. One envelope was postmarked May 10, Yr — 0. The other was postmarked May 25, Yr — 0. The envelopes contained letters beginning "Dear Arlo" and were signed "Mom." The May 10 letter discussed family matters, including a recounting by the author of a family reunion held on Easter Sunday. The letter went on to complain that the cost of the reunion was too great to be paid by the author alone.

Officers Making Report
/s/   **Nancy Mundy**
     Officer Nancy Mundy

SUPPLEMENTAL OFFENSE REPORT

The May 26 letter again made reference to the Easter reunion, this time thanking the addressee for agreeing to pay certain bills. Attached to the second letter was a bill from a restaurant indicating that $579.30 was owed for services provided on Easter, Yr — 0. A total of $3250 was found in the briefcase. Briefcase, envelopes, letters and bill were placed in reporting officer's evidence locker.

The film taken with the security camera shows the robber to be someone approximately 5'9" and 160 lbs. height and weight, person appears to be a white male, but the film only shows him from the back. No gun was found in vicinity of bank. Two tellers, Sherry Van Donk and Glenda Berg were questioned. Their statements are attached. Roy Smith was also questioned. Mr. Smith Roy was walking past the bank just as the robber was running out of the bank. Smith described the robber as between 5'8" and 5'10 and about 155. He was unable to describe the robber's face since the robber was still wearing the mask.

Nancy Mundy

STATEMENT OF SHERRY VAN DONK

My name is Sherry Van Donk and I am teller at First Investors. I've worked here for 6 months. Before that I was a teller with United Columbia Bank. I was at my window at about 1:30 when men walked up to me and said keep quiet and give me the money. He was carrying a big gun and was wearing a ski mask over his face. I gave him the money in the till and was able to also give him the money with the exploding stain. The device, hidden in the money and placed in the case, had a timer on it. The device is designed to explode, staining the money as the robber flees.

I'm sure he was a man from the way he walked and his voice. His hands were uncovered so I know he was white, but again, with the ski mask I couldn't see his face. I did, however, see that his eyes were blue. I'm 5'4" so he must have been about 5'10", maybe 170 lbs. He was wearing blue jeans, a green T shirt and a navy blue jacket; you know the light summer jacket thing.

Sherry Van Donk
Sherry Van Donk

STATEMENT OF GLENDA BERG

My name is Glenda Berg. I am senior teller at the bank. I've worked here for 3 years. I was working in the bank when a man came in. I first noticed him as he walked in the door. I thought someone was going to happen because he was carrying this hat and before I knew it he had pulled it over his head. I didn't get a real good view of his face. I guess I was kind of nervous and it was like only seconds between when I saw him come in the door and when he put the ski mask on. I immediately pressed the silent alarm and called Ms Dodge. The man went to Sherry's window first and then came to mine. He didn't say anything, just pointed that big gun at me and I gave him what money I had. Then he turned and ran away.

He was a white guy, I'd say in his late twenties, but that's just a guess. You know his shape made him look on the young side. He was about 35 feet away when he came in the door. He was maybe 5'9" or so and 160 lbs.

There were no other customers in the bank at the time.

Glenda Berg
Glenda Berg

IN THE CIRCUIT COURT OF
CALHOUN COUNTY
STATE OF COLUMBIA

THE STATE OF COLUMBIA
vs.

ARLO P. DUFFY,
Defendant.

No. CR Yr-0-464

INDICTMENT

THE GRAND JURY CHARGES:

On or about the first day of June, Yr-0, in the County of Calhoun, State of Columbia, Arlo Duffy committed the crime of

Armed Robbery

in violation of Section 18.2-93 of the Columbia Criminal Code in that he entered a First Investors Savings Bank, a bank, armed, with intent to commit larceny of money, bonds, notes, or other evidence of debt therein.

A TRUE BILL

Harry Shrag ,
Foreman of the Grand Jury

IN THE CIRCUIT COURT OF CALHOUN COUNTY STATE OF COLUMBIA

THE STATE OF COLUMBIA
vs.
ARLO P. DUFFY,
Defendant.

No. CR Yr-0-464

WARRANT FOR ARREST

To any authorized officer with authority and jurisdiction to execute a warrant for arrest for the offense charged below:

You are hereby commanded to arrest **Arlo P. Duffy** and bring him forthwith before the Circuit Court for the County of Calhoun, State of Columbia, to answer an indictment charging him with armed robbery of First Investors Savings Bank, in violation of Section 18.2-93 of the Columbia Criminal Code.

CLERK
By **Alice Stone**
Deputy Clerk.

IN THE CIRCUIT COURT OF
CALHOUN COUNTY
STATE OF COLUMBIA

THE STATE OF COLUMBIA
vs.
ARLO P. DUFFY,
Defendant.

No. CR Yr-0-464

SEARCH WARRANT

To any authorized officer with authority and jurisdiction to execute a search warrant:

Affidavit having been made before me by Jeffery Gorham that he has reason to believe that in the premises known as **Meadowbrook Apartments No. 219, 1300 Sheaf Ln, in Calhoun, Columbia**, there is now being concealed certain property, namely certain clothing and weapons used in the robbery of First Investors Savings Bank on June 1, and as the grand jury has indicted the occupant of these premises for the robbery of this bank on June 1, and as I am satisfied there is probable cause to believe that the property so described is being concealed on the premises above described,

You are hereby commanded to search the place named for the property specified, serving this warrant and making the search in the daytime, and if the property be found there to seize it, prepare a written inventory of the property seized and bring the property before me.

Dated: 6/5/Yr-0

A.L. Pickford
Circuit Court Judge

POLICE OFFICER'S ARREST REPORT
CALHOUN POLICE DEPARTMENT

ARRESTEE: Arlo Duffy   CHARGE: Armed Robbery

ADDRESS: 1300 Sheaff Ln.   PHONE: 555-3028

#219

DATE OF ARREST: 6/5/Yr-0   TIME OF ARREST 11:00 a.m.

DETAILS OF ARREST

Suspect was arrested without incident in his apartment at Meadowbrook Apartment No. 219. He was informed of his right to an attorney. Immediate search was made of the premises. Officer was unable to locate a firearm, ski mask, or green T shirt. Two pairs of blue jeans were seized. Following the search, suspect was removed to precinct where he was again informed of his right to an attorney. Suspect initially waived that right and voluntarily made a statement. This was done in the presence of arresting officer. After initially cooperating suspect asked for an attorney, and interrogation was suspended. Suspect through his attorney has refused to sign summary of statement made before suspect made request.

Copy of summary is attached to this report.

Jeffery Gorham

WITNESS STATEMENT
CALHOUN POLICE DEPARTMENT

STATEMENT OF ARLO DUFFY

DATE: 6/5/YR-0

TIME: 11:30 a.m.

My name is Arlo P. Duffy I live at Meadowbrook Apartments No. 219, 1300 Sheaf Ln, in Calhoun, Columbia. I know I have the right to an attorney, but I do not feel I need one because I am innocent. I am single, 33 year old, and have a college degree in English. I am presently employed as night manager at a local fast food restaurant, Roast Beef Delite. I have worked there for two years. Following graduation from college I was unable to get a job using my degree and therefore started working in a series of places: construction, landscaping and the like, but never held a job for more than one year. I have never served in the military.

My mother's name is Priscilla. She lives in Clinton, here in Columbia.

On June 1, I was at my mother's during the day. My father died 18 months ago and I try to get over to see mom at least twice a week. Sometimes that's hard, since she lives 60 miles away, but she gets lonely. I left about 9:00 a.m. and it took about 90 minutes to get to mom's. I stayed there until approximately 3:30 p.m. when I drove back to Calhoun. I went to my apartment, changed my clothes and was at work by 6:00 p.m. As usual, I worked until closing at midnight.

I do not own a gun. The briefcase shown to me by the officer looks like mine. It was stolen from my car on May 20, Yr-0. I think I better talk to a lawyer now, thank you.

Arlo Duffy
Jeffery Gorham
Officer Jeffery Gorham

Note: Mr. Duffy refused to sign. J.G.

Subscribed and sworn to before me this 5th day of June, Yr-0.

Notary Public

RED BARN FOOD CONCESSION

Food for all occasions
3568 Granger
Clinton, Columbia

Date: May 5, Yr-0

To: Priscilla Duffy
       125 Elm St.
       Clinton, Columbia

Quantity	Service/Item	Unit Cost	Total
70	Box Lunch	7.00	490.00
Subtotal			490.00
Tax			34.30
Service			55.00
Total			579.30

THANK YOU FOR ALLOWING US TO SERVE YOU

Customer Copy

From the Desk of

Priscilla Duffy

May 8, Yr-0

Dear Arlo,

We were all very sorry you were unable to make the family reunion on Easter. We had a wonderful time, and Aunt Shirley sends her love. These get togethers do make me miss your Dad, though.

Now the only problem is to figure out how to pay for it. Do you believe it cost almost $600! Outrageous! I'm really disappointed that no one asked to help to pay, not even Uncle Charlie. Well anyway, when are you coming to see me again? It's been three weeks and I do miss you.

Write! Love,

Mom

From the Desk of

Priscilla Duffy

May 23, Yr-0

Dear Arlo,

Just a note to say hi and thanks. Are you sure you can afford to pay this bill? The rest of the family should be ashamed of themselves, here you weren't even there.

Got to run, Alice and I are off to a garage sale.

Love,

Mom

222 Elm Street
Clinton, Columbia

Postmark
May 10, Yr.-0

Arlo Duffy
1300 Sheaff Lane, Apt 219
Calhoun, Columbia

222 Elm Street
Clinton, Columbia

Postmark
May 25, Yr.-0

Arlo Duffy
1300 Sheaff Lane, Apt 219
Calhoun, Columbia

RECORD OF ARREST
STATE POLICE
STATE OF COLUMBIA

Name: ARLO DUFFY   Date of Birth: 11/3/Yr-33
Social Security No.: 028-00-2800

Date	Address	Offense	Disposition
12/03/Yr-10	222 Elm Street Clinton, Columbia	Check Forgery (Felony)	Dismissed
09/01/Yr-6	222 Elm Street Clinton, Columbia	Grand Theft (Felony)	Guilty Plea to conspiracy to defraud (Misdemeanor) — 3 months state prison
08/24/Yr-4	1300 Sheaff Lane, Apt 219 Calhoun, Columbia	Indecent Exposure (Misdemeanor)	Conviction — 60 days County Jail — suspended
06/05/Yr-0	1300 Sheaff Lane, Apt 219 Calhoun, Columbia	Armed Robbery	Pending
06/05/Yr-0	1300 Sheaff Lane, Apt 219 Calhoun, Columbia	Armed Robbery	Pending

RELEVANT STATUTORY PROVISIONS

§ 18.2-93. Entering bank, armed, with intent to commit larceny.
— If any person, armed with a deadly weapon, shall enter any banking house, in the daytime or in the nighttime, with intent to commit larceny of money, bonds, notes, or other evidence of debt therein, he shall be guilty of a Class 2 felony.

§ 18.2-10. Punishment for conviction of felony.
— The authorized punishments for conviction of a felony are:

. . . .

(b) For Class 2 felonies, imprisonment for life or for any term not less than twenty years.

. . . .

§ 18.2-57. Robbery, defined.
— If any person takes, with the intent to deprive the owner permanently, property from the person of another, against his will, by violence or intimidation, upon conviction thereof he shall be guilty of robbery.

§ 18.2-58. Robbery, how Punished.
— If any person commit robbery by the threat or presenting of firearms, or other deadly weapon or instrumentality whatsoever, he shall be guilty of a felony and shall be punished by confinement in the penitentiary for life or any term not less than five years.

§ 18.2-94. Larceny; defined.
— If any person takes and carries away, with the intent to deprive the owner permanently, personal property belonging to another, without his assent, upon conviction thereof he shall be guilty of larceny.

§ 18.2-95. Grand larceny; how punished.
— Any person who:

(1) Commits larceny from the person of another of money or other thing of value of five dollars or more, or

(2) Commits simple larceny not from the person of another of goods and chattels of the value of $200 or more shall be deemed guilty of grand larceny which shall be punishable by confinement in the penitentiary for not less than one nor more than twenty years or in the discretion of the jury, or judge sitting without a jury, be confined jail for a period not exceeding twelve months or fined not more than $1000, either or both.

APPENDIX B

Donato v. Donato

This case involves a custody dispute between Gina and Paul Donato. Gina and Paul Donato were divorced three years ago. At that time, Gina received custody of the three children. The children are, Allen, eight, Ellen, 15, and Richard, 17.

In January, Yr-2, Gina enrolled in a night class at the local community college. The course, an introduction to computers, was a four-week mini-course meeting four hours a week. It was taught by Sam Gordon, a full time member of the community college faculty. A friendship developed between Sam and Gina. The friendship developed to the point where they began seeing each other every evening. On September, Yr-1, Gina lost her job. She collected unemployment, but had a hard time meeting her bills. In January, Yr-0, Sam suggested he move in with Gina and they could share expenses.

Richard disagreed with his mother's living arrangements and moved out of the house and into his father's apartment. It was then that Paul learned about Sam. As a result, Paul filed suit seeking custody of all three children.

Gina believes Paul loves the children, but is irresponsible and lives in a terrible apartment. For example, on August 15, Yr-1, a Saturday, Allen and Ellen went to a ball game with Paul. They planned to spend the night with their father. Around 10:00 p.m., when Allen was in bed, Paul went downstairs to a bar. It seems that Paul's apartment, owned by Matthew Vitti, is located over the Triangle Tavern. There was a thunderstorm and the roof apparently leaked. The suspended ceiling in the room where Allen was sleeping became soaked and fell in on him, cutting his head. Ellen called emergency number 911. Paul became aware of the problem when the police arrived at the apartment. Paul took Allen to the hospital emergency room. He received three stitches and went home with Gina, whom Paul had called. Gina has since refused to let the kids spend the night with Paul.

The state Domestic Relations Code provides:

§ 20-107.2. Determination of Custody — The court, in determining custody and visitation of minor children, shall consider the following:

1. The age and physical and mental condition of the child or children;

2. The age and physical and mental condition of each parent;

3. The relationship existing between each parent and each child;

4. The moral, intellectual, spiritual and physical needs of the child or children;

5. The role which each parent has played, and will play in the future, in the upbringing and care of the child or children;

6. Such other factors as are necessary to consider the best interests of the child or children.

§ 20-108 Presumptions — In awarding the custody of children to either parent, the court shall give primary consideration to the welfare of the child or children, and, as between parents, there shall be no presumption or inference in favor of either.

***

APPENDIX C

Paula v. David and Popular Dry Goods

Paula was driving her car to work on a June day, two years ago. As she approached the intersection of Libbie and Grove Avenues, she had a collision with David. David was driving a truck owned by his employer, Popular Dry Goods (PDG). Paula claims that she had the green light. David claims he had the green light. The accident was witnessed by two bystanders, Walter and Wanda.

Paula has retained Brewster Rawls, noted personal injury lawyer, to represent her. David and PDG are represented by noted defense counsel, Marla Graff.

Maple St.

Grove Ave.

N
W   E
S

Libbie Ave.

APPENDIX D

*In re Berger**

INSTRUCTIONS

1. You will have three hours to complete this session of the examination. This performance test is designed to evaluate your ability to handle a select number of legal authorities in the context of a factual problem involving a client.

2. The problem is set in the fictional state of Columbia, one of the United States. Your firm has been retained by Howard Berger to represent him in a contract for sale of land.

3. You will have two sets of materials with which to work: a File and a Library. You will be called upon to distinguish relevant from irrelevant facts, analyze the legal authorities provided, and prepare a memorandum.

4. The File contains factual information about your case in the form of seven documents. The first document is a memorandum to you from Jonathan Wright containing the instructions for the memorandum you are to prepare.

5. The Library includes Columbia statutes and four cases. The materials may be real, modified, or written solely for the purpose of this examination. Although the materials may appear familiar to you, do not assume that they are precisely the same cases you have read before. Read them thoroughly, as if all were new to you. You should assume that the cases were decided in the jurisdictions and on the dates shown.

6. Your memorandum must be written in the answer book provided. In answering this performance test, you should concentrate on the materials provided, but you should bring to bear on the problem your general knowledge of the law. What you have learned in law school and elsewhere provides the general background for analyzing the problem; the File and Library provide the specific materials with which you must work.

7. In citing cases from the Library, you may use abbreviations and delete citations.

8. Although there are no restrictions on how you apportion your time, you should probably allocate at least 90 minutes to organizing and writing your memorandum.

9. This performance test will be graded on your responsiveness to instructions and on content, thoroughness, and organization of the memoran-

---

* This performance test was originally administered by the Committee of Bar Examiners of the State Bar of California on February 23, 1993. The Performance Test is reproduced with the permission of the Committee.

dum you prepare. In gray the answers to this question, the following, approximate weights will be assigned to two parts of the memorandum:

Part A: 25%

Part B: 75%

FILE

Wright, Maddock & Rosenstock

Attorneys and Counselors at Law
658 Edgerton
Midlothian, Columbia

MEMORANDUM   February 23, Yr-0

To: Applicant

From: Jonathan Wright

Re: Berger Contract

Howard and Susan Berger have retained our firm to represent them in a matter arising out of a contract for the purchase of land. As will be clear from the file, the Bergers signed a contract for the purchase of about 40 acres of land on Lake Gaston. The Bergers' intent was to develop a campground on the property. Unfortunately, after the contract was signed, but before closing, the zoning on the property was changed. It will now be impossible to develop the campground, and the Bergers no longer want to go through with the purchase of the land.

I spoke with Mr. Berger on January 20 (an edited transcript of the interview is in the file), obtained a copy of the contract, and had some preliminary checking done at Lake Gaston. Based on that preliminary investigation, it now appears that the sellers, Peter and Helen Sloop, will be claiming title by adverse possession.

What I need to know is whether the Bergers will be held to the terms of the contract. If we can establish fraud, mutual mistake, or that title is not marketable, we may be able to rescind the contract or successfully defend an action for specific performance.

I have hired a private investigator, Johnny Ripka, to conduct the investigation of this case and want you to supervise his work. Write a memorandum to Ripka in which you do the following:

A.   Based upon your review of the legal materials I've gathered, briefly explain the elements of the applicable legal rules so that Ripka will know what to look for and why that information is important to the case. Remember that Ripka is a skilled investigator, but not a lawyer, so don't give him a legal brief or cite cases and statutes. Give him direction and guidance.

B.   More important, identify for Ripka possible facts that may relate to each element of the rules you stated in part A. Organize your memo to Ripka in the following way: (1) list each element of the rules you stated in part A; (2) under each element of the rules, specify the information you expect him to gather and how he should go about obtaining it. Remember, giving more detailed direction is better than giving less detail. For example, do not simply tell Ripka to seek all information available to establish whether Sloop's occupancy of the land has been "hostile." Instead, tell Ripka where he should go, whom he should interview, possible areas of inquiry, and what he should seek, including the potential testimonial, documentary, demonstrative, and physical evidence he should gather.

TRANSCRIPT OF INTERVIEW WITH HOWARD BERGER

Date: January 20, Yr-0

Time: 9:00 a.m.

Jonathan Wright (Attorney): Good morning, Mr. Berger. Won't you sit down?

Howard Berger (Mr. Berger): Thank you. Some building and office you have here.

Attorney: Thanks, we've just moved in. The firm was over on Applegate until the firm simply got too large for the offices. I hope you didn't have any trouble finding us.

Mr. Berger: No, not at all.

Attorney: Can I ask how you came to contact us?

Mr. Berger: Well, to be honest, I work just down the street and walk by here and noticed when you moved. I thought I'd give you a try.

Attorney: Great. I hope we're able to help you out. Why don't you tell me what we can do for you?

Mr. Berger: I've got a problem with the purchase of a piece of property. It turns out that what I wanted the property for I won't be able to do. So, I want to see if I can get out of the deal.

Attorney: Okay, let me see. Have you closed the transaction?

Mr. Berger: What do you mean?

Attorney: Have you taken the deed to the property?

Mr. Berger: Oh, no. That's what I want to avoid. You see, I wanted to open this recreation, campground kind of area down on Lake Gaston, and now they've gone and zoned the property residential. It doesn't look like I'll be able to use it the way I want to.

Attorney: I see. Do you have a written contract with the seller?

Mr. Berger: Yes. In fact, I brought it with me. That newspaper clipping there is how I found out about the zoning change.

Attorney: Fine. I'll read these in a second. First, why don't we start at the beginning of your contract with, let's see, the contract says the seller's name is Peter Sloop.

Mr. Berger: Well, you see, my wife and I have been going down to Lake Gaston for about two years now. We've got this 18-foot power boat and we drive the 100 miles or so down there on weekends. That's a bit of a ways, so we thought we might try camping, but we couldn't find any place to do that, and the nearest motel to the lake is about thirty miles. Well, that got us to thinking that maybe there was some money to be made setting up a campground. It just so happens my father is looking to retire and had mentioned that he

	might like to run a campground, and I thought, gee, maybe that's the thing. My wife and I could buy some land, set up a campground, and then let my father run it.
Attorney:	I see. It's interesting there are no campgrounds on Gaston. I thought that it was a pretty big lake.
Mr. Berger:	Oh, it is. I'd guess it's 25 miles long and 5 miles wide at parts. I don't know if you know it or not, but about 15 years ago the Columbia Power Company dammed the Staunton River, making Lake Gaston. It's a real rural area. The Power Company bought most of the land, built the dam, and flooded the area. Over the past 15 years or so there has been slow but steady development of some residential areas, but I'd guess that at least 80 percent of the shoreline still borders farms or forest. Of course, the roads are all two-lane and there is only one bridge across the lake. It is pretty inconvenient to get to various parts of the lake. The lake bottom is owned by the Power Company. In fact, I'm told you need the Power Company's permission to put a dock in the lake.
Attorney:	So, getting back to your plans, how long ago did you come up with the idea?
Mr. Berger:	About 18 months ago, we started going to real estate agents down there. They don't have multiple listings, so you have to deal with a lot of little real estate offices. Well, after about six months we were pretty discouraged. The prices they were asking were just outrageous. A waterfront lot goes for 25 to 30 thousand dollars for maybe three-quarters acre and 160 feet of waterfront. Now all I really needed was about 200 feet of waterfront, but maybe 20 to 30 acres. I just couldn't find that kind of pie-shaped property and I couldn't afford to piece it together with individual lots.
Attorney:	So what did you do?
Mr. Berger:	About six months ago, we were down at Gaston just driving around. We had brought the boat down, but then it started to rain so we packed up and headed for home. Since it was early, we decided to go a different way home and headed west. After a while we came to a diner and decided to stop for a soda. We were sitting in a booth, I guess complaining a little bit about our bad luck. The guy behind the counter comes up and says he's not sure, but that he thinks this guy Sloop may be interested in selling his farm, and he thinks it is maybe 40 acres but it has only a little bit of waterfront. Well, I figure it's worth a try, so we head out to take a look. Took us a bit of a while to find the place since it was off the paved state highway about two miles, but that was fine, since you had to go through some rolling farmland and then some forest, which would give the campers an added sense of being out in the wild. Eventually the road dead ended at Sloop's place and, to make a long story short, the place was perfect — 40 acres and only 400 feet of waterfront.

Attorney:	Did you talk to Sloop then?
Mr. Berger:	No, but we located him and set up a meeting.
Attorney:	What happened then?
Mr. Berger:	I explained what my wife and I were interested in doing, really the same stuff I told you, and asked if he was interested in selling. He said he might, but he'd have to think about it and discuss it with his wife. He agreed that the property would make an ideal campground.
Attorney:	What happened then?
Mr. Berger:	What with business and things, we didn't get back in touch with Sloop until maybe a month later. I had tried to call him but couldn't get a phone listing, so we just waited until the next weekend we were able to get down there. We talked and he said that he had given it a lot of thought and that he would be willing to sell.
Attorney:	Did he say why?
Mr. Berger:	Seems he'd been on the place for only about three years; said he'd inherited it from his uncle when he died. His uncle had retired to the property after working at the grain elevator over in Littleton. That's the major town on Gaston. Major, that's a joke. It's about 3000 people. Really four corners with a grocery store, café, library, bank, gas station, feed store, grain elevator, and combination community center and town hall. Anyway, Sloop said he just never was able to take full advantage of the land since he worked in town managing the grocery store as well as working nights at the café in Littleton. He said it ought to be turning a profit in grain or livestock, but he just didn't have the time to make a real go of it.
Attorney:	Did you make the deal then?
Mr. Berger:	Yes. I had gotten a form contract from a real estate agent friend of mine a couple of years ago when I'd thought about selling our house here in Midlothian. I'd taken the form down to Gaston with me. After Sloop agreed to sell, we went to the diner and negotiated the deal that you see in the contract. The price was higher than I expected, but I think he knew that I really wanted the property for the campground.
Attorney:	I see.
Mr. Berger:	Well, what do you think? Can I get out of the deal?
Attorney:	At this point, I don't know. Let me ask you this, isn't the property worth more as residential?
Mr. Berger:	You might think that. In fact, I contacted a real estate agent but was told with the limited waterfront most of the land was really not appropriate for residential development. People want to be on the water, or there's really no point in being there. It's so far from

everything that few people are going to pay lots of money to have a primary residence there, especially one not on the lake. So, what do you think?

Attorney: To be honest, I don't know. I'm going to have to look at this contract very carefully and then do some research and perhaps some investigation. I can tell you we'll do our best. What I'd need to do is take a week to look into the matter and then meet with you again. Let me ask you something first. Have you spoken to Mr. Sloop? Perhaps he would simply call the deal off.

Mr. Berger: No, not really.

Attorney: The reason I ask is that this is not going to be cheap and perhaps you could resolve this with a phone call.

Mr. Berger: How much?

Attorney: My fee is $120 per hour. I would estimate that just the preliminary work will take six hours. In addition, I'll need to contact a law firm in Littleton to do some brief preliminary investigation. I would estimate that would cost $250. It just seems that before you incur that cost, a phone call would be worth a try.

Mr. Berger: I guess you're right. I'll run down there and see.

Attorney: Good. I'll hold off for what, a week? If you can talk to Sloop in that time, give me a call and we can decide how to proceed.

Mr. Berger: Fine, I'll call you one week from today.

Attorney: Oh, by the way, see if you can get a plat or drawing of the property, would you? That would be helpful.

Mr. Berger: Sure.

CONTRACT FOR THE SALE OF LAND

This agreement, made this 20ᵗʰ day of December , Yr -1 between Peter Sloop and Helen Sloop , husband and wife, residing at Littleton, Columbia , herein called the Seller, and Howard Berger and Susan Berger , husband and wife, residing at Coalfield Rd., Midlothian, CO herein called the Buyer.

1. Sale. The Seller agrees to sell and convey and the Buyer agrees to buy:

(a) All that certain plot, piece, or parcel of land, with the buildings and improvements thereon, situated, lying and being in the City of Gaston , County , generally known as xxxxxxxxxx , herein called the Premises and more particularly described as: [here describe].

> 40 acres more or less owned by Peter Sloop on the north shore of Lake Gaston located between state routes 613 and 645 and entered of route 613

(b) All the plumbing, heating, lighting and cooking fixtures, bathroom and kitchen cabinets, automatic dishwashers, carpets, linoleum, Venetian blinds, window shades, curtain rods, awnings, screens, storm windows, storm doors, radio and television aerials, window boxes, mail boxes, fences, clothes lines, and all other fixtures attached or appurtenant to the Premises.

(c) The following items of personal property located on or used in connection with the Premises: [here list the items to be sold].

None

2. Purchase Price. The Buyer agrees to pay for the above described real and personal property the sum of $ 140,000 as follows:

$ 5,000 , on the signing of this contract, by check subject to collection, the receipt of which is hereby acknowledged;

$ 135,000 , in cash or good certified check on the delivery of the deed as hereinafter provided.

3. Title. The title to be delivered shall be a marketable title and insurable by a Title Company and shall be free and clear of all encumbrances including municipal liens and assessments and liability for assessments for improvements now constructed (except as herein stated), this clause to be operative as of the date of this agreement, and the title is to be subject to all existing restrictions of record. The Seller, however, guarantees that there are no restrictions in any conveyance or plans of record affecting the premises which will prohibit the use or occupancy thereof as a dwelling.

4. Exceptions to Title. The Premises are sold and are to be conveyed subject to:

(a) Reservations, restrictions, and easements of record.

(b) Applicable zoning regulations and ordinances.

(c) Real property taxes and assessments for the current year.

(d) Any state of facts an accurate survey may show.

5. Apportionments. The following items are to be apportioned, as of the date of closing:

(a) Real property taxes for the year in which the closing takes place.

(b) Premiums on any policies of insurance taken over by the Buyer.

(c) Rents, if such property is occupied by tenants at the date of the closing.

(d) Interest on the first mortgage.

(e) Water and sewer charges.

6. Possession. Possession of the Premises shall be delivered by the Buyer upon delivery of the deed. Time is of the essence of this contract.

7. Assessments. All assessments for local improvements now a lien or which may become a lien prior to the closing shall be paid by the Seller.

8. Deed. The deed shall be the usual bargain and sale deed in proper statutory form for record, and shall be duly executed and acknowledged so as to convey to the Buyer the fee simple of the premises, free of all encumbrances, except as herein stated.

9. Date and Place of Closing. The deed shall be delivered upon receipt of the payment of the purchase price as herein provided at the offices of __a__ Title Company, _to be determined_ at _____ o'clock, M.., on _March 20_, Yr-_0_. The Seller, however, shall have the right to adjourn the closing ~~to~~ _for good reason_ ~~19 upon giving the Buyer notice of such effect on or before, Yr.~~

10. Surviving Covenants. No provision of this contract survives the delivery of the deed except as expressly provided. Acceptance of the deed shall be an acceptance of all of the obligations of the Seller hereunder except such as may expressly be stated to survive the delivery of the deed.

11. ~~Broker. The Buyer represents that the only broker he has authorized to act on his behalf in respect to this transaction is~~ _____, and that the Buyer has not authorized any other broker to submit any offer his behalf to the Seller to purchase the Premises. The Buyer shall indemnify and save the Seller harmless from any claim by any broker (other than _____) that he was authorized on behalf of the Buyer to make an offer to the Seller in respect of this transaction. The representations contained in this paragraph shall survive delivery of the deed.

12. Successors. This contract shall extend to and be binding upon the heirs, administrators, executors, successors, and assigns of the respective parties hereto.

13. Entire Agreement. This contract constitutes the entire agreement between the parties.

In Witness Whereof, this contract has been signed, sealed, and delivered the day and year first above written.

Fred Mills
Witness

Howard Berger
Susan Berger
Peter Sloop
Helen Sloop

The Littleton Gazette, January 15, Yr-0

Supervisors Take Action
On Land and Cats

County supervisors last night, following weeks of intense conflicting pressure, adopted Gaston County's first zoning ordinance change since the creation of Lake Gaston. In an action many feel is just the first step in controlling development on Lake Gaston, the supervisors rezoned as residential the entire area bounded by the north shore of the lake and state routes 645 and 613.

In other actions, the supervisors adopted an ordinance requiring rabies vaccinations for all cats. Previously, only dogs were required to be vaccinated. Dr. William Bradford, Director of the County Health Department, was quoted as saying, "This will go a long way in curbing the increasing number of rabies cases within the county."

Wright, Maddock & Rosenstock

Attorneys and Counselors at Law
658 Edgerton
Midlothian, Columbia

MEMORANDUM   January 27, Yr-0

To: File

From: Jonathan Wright

Re: Berger Fife

I spoke with Mr. Berger today. He indicated he spoke with Sloop and explained his problem with closing on the property. Sloop was firm about holding the Bergers to the contract. Mr. Berger asked Sloop if he had a survey of the land and Sloop said no. Sloop explained that his uncle hadn't gotten the property in a formal way, but that his uncle's lawyer had told his uncle that it did not matter. Mr. Berger said Sloop indicated he had the property "by adversity or something."

Mr. Berger said Sloop told him the uncle was apparently a bit of a recluse, stayed pretty much to himself, except the occasional visit to the grocery store and his weekly trip to church.

In light of that conversation, we agreed I should proceed with the investigation of the Bergers' rights.

Williams and Harold

Attorneys at Law
Littleton, Columbia

February 8, Yr-0

Jonathan Wright
Wright, Maddock and Rosenstock
658 Edgerton
Midlothian, Columbia

Dear Jonathan:

As per our phone conversation of January 27 and your letter of that same date enclosing a contract, I have undertaken your two requests, searching the title to the property and inquiring as to the zoning of the property.

First, as to the zoning, your client was correct in his fears concerning the zoning change. The zoning of the property described in the contract was indeed part of that affected by the supervisors' actions of January 14, and the zoning would clearly prohibit use of the land as a campground. I must admit, this did not require a great deal of investigation. The rezoning of that particular area of the county has been a major subject of debate for close to a year now.

Your second request raised more interesting questions. Interestingly, a title search failed to uncover any deed in which Sloop is a grantee. There was a probated will in which Sloop was named as grantee of the property from one Arnold Rudy, apparently an uncle of Sloop's. Rudy died three years ago. Surprisingly, there is also no record of Arnold Rudy as grantee of the land.

I hope this has been of assistance. If we can be of further help, please let me know. A statement for services will arrive under separate cover.

Cordially,
Jerold Williams
Jerold Williams

JUDITH DANIELS

Attorney
Littleton, Columbia

February 9, Yr-0

Howard and Susan Berger
121 Coalfield Road
Midlothian, Columbia

Dear Mr. and Mrs. Berger:

Mr. Peter Sloop has consulted me concerning the contract for the sale of land signed by you and Mr. Sloop December 20, Yr-1. Mr. Sloop informed me of his discussion with you January 25 and fears you intend to breach that contract.

Having reviewed the contract, I have advised Mr. Sloop that you are legally obliged to close the contract on March 20, Yr-0. Mr. Sloop has decided he expects you to abide by the terms of the contract and will take all steps to protect his legal rights.

If you are represented by an attorney, please forward this letter to him or her.

Sincerely,
Judith Daniels
Judith Daniels

LIBRARY

Columbia Code of Civil Procedure

§ 322. When it appears that the occupant, or those under whom he claims, entered into the possession of the property under claim of title, exclusive of other right, founding such claim upon a written instrument, as being a conveyance of the property in question, or upon the decree or judgment of a competent court, and that there has been a continued occupation and possession of the property included in such instrument, decree, or judgment, of some part of the property, under such claim, for five years, the property so included is deemed to have been held adversely, except that when it consists of a tract divided into lots, the possession of one lot is not deemed a possession of any other lot of the same tract.

§ 323. For the purpose of constituting an adverse possession by any person claiming a title, founded upon a written instrument, or a judgment or decree, land is deemed to have been possessed and occupied in the following cases:

1. Where it has been usually cultivated or improved;

2. Where it has been protected by a substantial enclosure;

3. Where, although not enclosed, it has been used for the supply of fuel, or of fencing-timber for the purposes of husbandry, or for pasturage, or for the ordinary use of the occupant;

4. Where a known farm or single lot has been partly improved, the portion of such farm or lot that may have been left not cleared, or not enclosed according to the usual course and custom of the adjoining country, shall be deemed to have been occupied for the same length of time as the part improved and cultivated.

§ 324. Where it appears that there has been actual continued occupation of land, under a claim of title, exclusive of any other right, but not founded upon a written instrument, judgment, or decree, the land so actually occupied, and no other, is deemed to have been held adversely.

§ 325. For the purpose of constituting an adverse possession by a person claiming title not founded upon a written instrument, judgment, or decree, land is deemed to have been possessed and occupied in the following cases only:

First — Where it has been protected by a substantial enclosure.

Second — Where it has been usually cultivated or improved.

Provided, however, that in no case shall adverse possession be considered established under the provisions of any section or sections of this Code, unless it shall be shown that the land has been occupied and claimed for the period of five years continuously, and the party or persons, their predecessors and grantors, have paid all the taxes, state, county, or municipal, which have been levied and assessed upon such land.

Colin v. Davidson
Columbia Supreme Court (1968)

Plaintiffs, buyers, contracted to buy from defendants, sellers, a residential property in Ridgewood. The purchasers refused to consummate the sale, alleging defects in title and misrepresentations on the part of the sellers. Plaintiffs instituted an action for rescission, and defendants counterclaimed for specific performance.

At the conclusion of the purchasers' case, the court granted the sellers' motion for judgment. The purchasers appealed; the Appellate Division ordered that judgment be entered in favor of the purchasers. Although we agree with the Appellate Division that the trial court erred in granting sellers' motion, we think its entry of judgment in purchasers' favor to have been clearly erroneous. There must be a new trial since the sellers have not had an opportunity to present evidence supporting their case.

Since there must be a new trial, it may be helpful for us to comment upon certain statements and contentions appearing in the opinions filed below as well as in the briefs. Because the sellers have had no opportunity to present their case, some of the facts we here assume necessarily rest upon inference if not conjecture.

It would appear that the validity of the title to a portion of the premises in question is sought to be sustained by the sellers upon a claim of adverse possession. The purchasers take the position that this being so, they were justified in repudiating the agreement; that the sellers could not force such a title upon them but should have perfected the record title prior to the date of closing. This, they add, should have been done either by securing a deed from the present record title holder, or by means of an action to quiet title. While we readily concede that the sellers would have been well advised to have followed such a course, we do not agree that their failure to do so imperiled their position to the extent urged by the purchasers. When a prospective seller's title is grounded upon adverse possession, or contains some apparent flaw of record, he has a choice of options. He may at once take whatever steps are necessary to perfect the record title, including resort to an action to quiet title, an action to cancel an outstanding encumbrance, or whatever other appropriate step may be necessary to accomplish the purpose. In the alternative, he may, believing his title to be marketable despite the fact that it rests on adverse possession or is otherwise imperfect of record, choose to enter into a contract of sale, hoping to convince 'the purchaser or, if necessary, a court, that his estimate of the marketability of his title is justified. That is the course the sellers seem to have followed here. It must be borne in mind that this latter course is available only where the contract of sale does not require the vendor to give a title valid of record, but provides for a less stringent requirement, such as marketability or insurability. Such is the case here. Here the contract contained the following provision:

> Title to be conveyed shall be marketable and insurable, at regular rates, by any reputable title insurance company licensed to do business in the State of Columbia, subject only to the encumbrances herein above set forth.

It will be seen at once that while the title for which the purchasers have contracted must be marketable and insurable, there is no requirement that it be a perfect title of record. Many titles, imperfect of record, are nonetheless marketable. Justice Cardozo, then Chief Judge of the New York Court of Appeals, observed:

> The law assures to a buyer a title free from reasonable doubt, but not from every doubt . . . If the only defect in the title is a very remote and improbable contingency, a slender possibility only, a conveyance will be decreed.

Incidentally, the law will imply that title must be marketable, even where the contract is silent upon the point. The purchasers are accordingly in error in insisting that nothing less than a good record title will suffice. A title that is marketable and insurable, though imperfect of record, will meet the terms of the contract.

The purchasers also advance the contention that the validity of the title must be assessed as of the specified closing date, and not at some later time. But established doctrine refutes this contention. Where, because of an alleged title defect, vendor and vendee litigate the issue, it will be the title as it exists at the time of final decree or judgment that will control, not the title the vendor may have had when the suit was commenced.

To recapitulate, in an action for specific performance by a seller or for rescission by a purchaser, where the issue is marketability of title, the seller is entitled to a judgment if, at the conclusion of the suit, the court holds title to be marketable, even though the decision in favor of marketability rests upon facts adduced for the first time at trial or upon legal rulings made during the course of the proceedings.

As we have said, we agree with the Appellate Division that the trial court erred in granting the sellers' motion at the conclusion of the purchasers' case. The purchasers had shown that the sellers did not have record title to one tract of the entire parcel. The contract of sale provided that title must be marketable and insurable. It did not provide, however, as many such agreements do, that the sellers would be required to produce a clear title of record, without reliance upon adverse possession. It is well settled in Columbia that title resting in adverse possession, if clearly established, will be held marketable. This rule represents the great weight of authority. Accordingly, if the sellers could prove that they did in fact hold title to the tract in question by virtue of adverse possession, they would have met their contractual obligation, at least insofar as marketability is concerned.

We note that it is not necessary for the sellers to join as parties all claimants with possible adverse interests, as would be the case in an action to quiet title. In many, if not most, cases of this sort the claimants who may hold adverse interests are not joined; very often they are not known. It follows, as the purchasers here correctly point out, that a judgment in the action will not be *res judicata* as to such claimants. And yet, virtually all courts agree that in such a suit there may be, and often is, a judgment of marketability leading to affirmative relief by way of specific performance or to a denial of a purchaser's claim to rescind. In order to reach this result, the court must conclude (1) that the claimants could not succeed were they in fact to assert a claim, (2) that there is no real likelihood that any claim will ever be asserted. Such a conclusion leads to a determination of marketability.

The judgment of the Appellate Division entering judgment in favor of the purchasers is reversed and the cause is remanded for a new trial in accordance with what has been said above.

Newman Lumber Company v Cornelius
Columbia Supreme Court (1970)

This action in quiet title involves lands in the mountains of Sierra County. Respondents asserted ownership by adverse possession pursuant to Code of Civil Procedure section 322 and its companion section 323. The judgment awarded respondents title to their several claims.

Between 1932 and 1950, the predecessors in interest of the several respondents entered upon the land and took up mining claims. The respondent parties to this action purchased their respective mining claims between 1952 and 1962 and received quitclaim deeds. Thus, some of the respondents have occupied the land without interruption for more than twenty years, all for more than five years.

All respondents believed they occupied land owned by the United States, and between 1932 and 1950 had received quitclaim deeds for mining claims. They located their claims, did their discovery work, recorded notices of location and annual proofs of labor, all as required by state and federal laws for locating mining claims upon public lands. They improved the property by the construction of one- to three-room cabins and miscellaneous other structures, such as outhouses and chicken coops. They also did some road work. Due to severe weather conditions, the several properties were inaccessible in winter by ordinary and usual means. During the spring and summer, some respondents spend every other weekend on the property, and one has resided there since 1961. During the winter, the latter gets in and out once a week with a four-wheel drive vehicle, aided by shoveling.

Examining each of the five requirements for adverse possession in relation to the evidence, and with particular reference to appellant's contention that respondents' occupation was not hostile to the appellant, we observe and hold:

(1) *Actual occupation.* This is not disputed.

(2) *Hostile possession.* The requirement of hostility means, not that the parties must have a dispute as to the title during the period of possession or that there is open aggression or combat, but that the claimant's possession must be adverse to the record owner, unaccompanied by any recognition, express or inferable from the circumstances, of the right in the latter. The possession must not only operate as an ouster of the holder of the legal title, but the title must be claimed as against the true owner during the entire statutory period.

Thus, it has been held that one who occupies the land of another in the mistaken belief that he, and not some other person, is the owner, doing so openly for the statutory period, and paying all taxes levied against the land, acquires title by adverse possession. We hold that respondents' mistaken belief that the United States owned the land was not a bar to their holding adversely as against all others, including appellant.

(3) *Claim to property under color of title.* Respondents' claims are founded upon written instruments, i.e., quitclaim deeds. Appellant contends respondents do not have color of title since their quitclaim deeds from the United States

conveyed mineral rights, not the entire fee simple. The grantee, under a deed quitclaiming to him all rights of the grantor to mine land, acquires at least color of title which can ripen into actual title by adverse possession of the underlying fee. This assumes, of course, an absence of fraud or bad faith. In any event, were the court to adopt appellant's contention, it would not lead to a different result since, applying all other elements of this analysis, respondents would likewise prevail under Code sections 324 and 325.

(4) *Continuous and uninterrupted possession for five years.* Respondents' occupation was uninterrupted for well over five years prior to 1958. The property is in a mountainous area, virtually inaccessible except in the spring and the summer. The evidence is that the respondents went upon their premises during the spring and summer of each year, residing thereon for two or three days, and sometimes longer, on each visit. If but slight use can be made of land claimed adversely, then the requirements of continuous and uninterrupted occupancy are satisfied, if such slight use as can be made is made thereof.

We hold that the requirement of continuous and uninterrupted possession for five years has been met.

(5) *Payment of all taxes levied against the property.* The only taxes levied in connection with the property prior to 1958 were the possessory interest taxes levied on the named mining claims of the respondents. These were paid by them. No real property taxes were levied until after 1958. Therefore, respondents paid all taxes levied prior to 1958.

Appellant lumber company's contention that respondents have forfeited whatever interest they claim in appellant's land because the lumber company, and not respondents, has paid all taxes levied on the real property since 1958 is without merit for this reason: respondents, or some of them, acquired the right to occupy the land described in their respective notices of location by adverse possession prior to 1958. They continued in uninterrupted physical possession to the time of trial.

The judgment is affirmed.

Donato v. Reliance Standard Life Insurance Company
Pennsylvania Supreme Court (1969)

On August 4, 1965, the Reliance Standard Life Insurance Company (Reliance) entered into an Agreement of Sale with Anthony and Viola Donato. Under the terms of the contract, Reliance agreed to sell to the appellants for $16,000 the premises located at 1015–23 South 3rd Street, Philadelphia. Reliance executed a certification stating that the premises were zoned industrial. This certification was correct and was appended to the Agreement of Sale.

On September 22, 1965, an ordinance was enacted which changed the zoning of the subject premises from G-2 Industrial to R10 Residential. Not until November 9, 1965, however, did the public records note this change.

In 1967, the Donatos contracted to sell the subject premises and then learned for the first time of the zoning change. After unsuccessfully seeking a variance, the appellants brought an equity action against Reliance to rescind the Agreement of Sale of August 4, 1965.

The question presented is one of first impression in Pennsylvania. However, it is well-established law here that when the Agreement of Sale is signed, the purchaser becomes the equitable or beneficial owner through the doctrine of equitable conversion: The vendor retains merely a security interest for the payment of the unpaid purchase money. It is also the law of Pennsylvania that the purchaser of real estate bears the risk of loss for injury occurring to the property after execution of the Agreement of Sale but before settlement.

In resolving the question here, we are aided by the thinking of Professor Arthur Linton Corbin, who enunciates the general rule as follows:

> After a contract for the sale of land has been made, but before actual conveyance, it sometimes happens that a zoning ordinance is adopted limiting the uses to which the property may be put. For example, it may be restricted to residences only, so that warehouses, garages, and the like are excluded. This change in the law may frustrate in part or in whole the purpose for which the purchaser agreed to buy the land. In the absence of some expression in the contract to the contrary, the risk of such a restriction by ordinance seems likely to be allocated to the purchaser.

There appears to be no cogent argument for treating losses resulting from zoning changes occurring between the execution of the Agreement of Sale and settlement differently from casualty and other kinds of loss occurring between those periods. The parties are always free to mold rights and responsibilities inter se in whatever fashion they desire. But when they are quiet, the law will speak in a voice of finality to set their dispute to rest.

Decree affirmed.

Clay v. Landreth
Virginia Supreme Court (1986)

Pearl C. Clay filed this complaint against the defendants, Landreth and Tysinger, the purpose of which was to have the court decree the specific performance of a certain contract made between the parties for the sale and purchase of a certain lot. The trial court denied the relief requested.

The defense set forth in the answer was that the parties agreed to sell and purchase the lot for the purpose of erecting a storage plant for ice cream and frozen fruits, at a time when the particular use was not prohibited by the zoning ordinances of the City of Roanoke. It was averred that between the time the contract was made and the time for the delivery of the deed, the city council rezoned this lot so that it could be used only for residence purposes; that at the time of making the contract it was contemplated and known by both the vendor and the vendee that it was to be used for the purpose of erecting a storage plant for ice cream and frozen fruits; that the rezoning of the lot has caused a very substantial depreciation in its value; that it would be inequitable and produce results not within the intent or understanding of the parties when the contract was made if specific performance should be decreed; and that to enforce the contract under such circumstances would be harsh and oppressive to the defendants.

The appellant argues here that the doctrine of equitable conversion applies; that this court should consider done what ought to have been done; and that in equity the complainant or vendor should be considered the owner of the purchase money and the defendants or vendees the owners of the lot as of the date of the contract. The resultant loss of the intended use of the property and the loss in value of the lot sustained by the rezoning would fall on the defendants if this theory were applied.

That the doctrine of equitable conversion exists in Virginia cannot be doubted. The rule, however, is limited in its application to cases where the enforcement of the contract is in accord with the intention of the parties, free from fraud, misrepresentation and the like, and where it will not produce inequitable results. Equitable conversion will not be applied if, by doing so, hardship and injustice are forced upon one of the parties through a change in circumstances not contemplated by them when the contract was made. This equitable principle applies equally whether the case involves a will or a contract for the sale of land.

Where specific performance is asked as well as where reformation of an instrument is sought on the ground of mutual mistake, and where the element of hardship and injustice comes into the case through a change in circumstances not contemplated by the parties when the contract-was entered into, the relief will not be granted.

If something has intervened which ought to prevent it, the doctrine of equitable conversion will not be applied. It does not exist as a matter of right and is not applicable to all circumstances. It is a fiction invented by courts of equity to be applied only when necessity and justice require its exercise. When it arises from a contract, as distinguished from a will, the general rule is that the legal fiction is based upon the presumed intent of the parties.

When the agreed facts are considered, it is apparent that, in the case at bar, the legal fiction of equitable conversion should not be applied because to do so would set at naught the intent and purpose of the parties with resultant hardship and injustice to the defendants. The sole intent of the vendor in the contract was to sell to the vendees a lot for the erection of a storage plant and the vendees intended to purchase a lot usable for the erection of a storage plant. This intent has been defeated by the supervening act of the council of Roanoke in rezoning the property, which has effected such a substantial change of conditions and loss in value that it would be inequitable to apply the doctrine of equitable conversion.

Of course, if a contract is certain and unambiguous, based upon a valuable consideration, free from fraud or mistake, not unconscionable, and its performance will not result in oppression upon the defendant, as a matter of course it will be specifically performed in equity; but on the other hand, if the circumstances and conditions have been so changed since its execution as to impose a loss and injustice upon an innocent defendant, a court of equity ordinarily will not enforce it regardless of the plaintiff's freedom from fault.

In *Anderson v. Stairway & Sons*, specific performance was refused in a New York case almost identical with the one at bar because it would have been inequitable to have required performance. The court ruled that neither party to the contract when it was made could have reasonably anticipated that before closing the transaction the lawmaking power would step in and impose such restrictions upon the use of the property as would render it useless to the defendant for the only purpose for which he sought to acquire it. Like considerations obtain in the case at bar. From our research the logical and sound principle announced in Anderson is still the law of New York.

In Williston on Contracts, the author states, in speaking of zoning ordinances, that "if a restriction precludes use of the land for the purpose for which, as the vendor knows, it is bought, specific performance will not be granted."

What has been quoted is sufficient to show that a court of equity may refuse specific performance when a subsequent change of circumstances not contemplated by the parties, occurring after the contract has been made, would render it inequitable.

Finally, the appellant contends that the defendants were guilty of fraud in that they did not disclose the potential rezoning of the lot in question. Defendants denied knowledge of the proposed zoning change. The trial court held, and we affirm, that defendants' knowledge was irrelevant to the fraud issue. Even were the court to find defendant was aware of the proposed zoning change prior to signing the contract, defendant was under no obligation to disclose affirmatively matters of governmental action or public knowledge.

The intervening of governmental authority has vitiated the purpose which was the foundation for the contract. It rendered the property useless to the defendants in that they could not use it for the intended purpose. The complainant cannot convey to the defendants what they agreed to purchase and he agreed to convey.

We think the decree should be affirmed.

APPENDIX E

*Dodson v. Canadian Equipment Company** *

INSTRUCTIONS

A. You will have 90 minutes to complete this session of the examination. This performance test is designed to evaluate your ability to handle a select number of legal authorities in the context of a factual problem involving a client.

B. The problem is set in the fictional state of Columbia, one of the United States. Columbia is located within the fictional United States Court of Appeals for the Fifteenth Circuit.

C. You will have two sets of material with which to work: A File and a Library. The File contains factual information about your case. The first document is a memorandum containing the instructions for the tasks you are to complete.

D. The Library contains the legal authorities needed to complete the tasks. Any cases may be real, modified, or written solely for the purpose of this examination. If the cases appear familiarity to you, do not assume that they are precisely the same as you have read before. Read them thoroughly, as if all were new to you. You should assume that cases were decided in the jurisdictions and on the dates shown. In citing cases from the Library, you may use abbreviations and omit citations.

E. Your response must be written in the answer book provided. In answering this performance test, you should concentrate on the materials provided, but you should also bring to bear on the problem of your general knowledge of the laws. What you have learned in law school and elsewhere provides the general background for analyzing the problem; the File and Library provide the specific materials with which you must work.

F. Although there are no restrictions on how you apportion your time, you should probably allocate at least 45 minutes to organizing and writing.

G. This performance test will be graded on your responsiveness to instructions and on the content, thoroughness, and organization of your response.

---

* This performance test was originally administered by the Committee of Bar Examiners of the State Bar of California on July 29, 1993. The Federal Rules of Evidence contained in the library are updated in light of changes since that date. The Performance Test is reproduced with the permission of the Committee.

FILE

Freeman, Duke and Woolridge
3000 Paragon Place
Frederick, Columbia

MEMORANDUM   July 29, Yr-0

To: Applicant

From: Elizabeth Duke

Re: <u>Dodson v Canadian Equipment Company</u>

I need your help preparing for the trial in this case. As you may know, we represent the plaintiff, Esther Dodson, in this product liability action arising out of an automobile accident in which our client was the driver and her sister, Denise Johnston, was a passenger. Denise claims she was' injured in the accident, and we have reason to believe that Denise intends later to sue Esther for negligence.

We've brought suit under negligence and strict product liability theories against Canadian Equipment Company (CEC), the manufacturer of Esther's car. Basically, our claim is that CEC is liable for Esther's injuries (she was rendered paraplegic) caused by shattered glass from the sunroof which was manufactured from tempered glass, a product that is inferior to laminated glass. If laminated glass had been used, it would not have shattered and Esther's cervical nerves would not have been severed. We have a serious problem, however, on the negligence claim, because CEC claims that our client was not wearing a seat belt. If that fact is established, the contributory negligence laws in Columbia will preclude recovery under a negligence theory. That makes our strict liability theory all the more important because contributory negligence will not bar it.

Critical to our negligence claim will be the testimony of Esther's sister. Esther tells us she has been estranged from her sister for many years. The primary cause of friction between them is "Denise's behavior." Esther does not have details, but is aware that Denise has several criminal convictions. Although Esther has been critical of her sister, she has attempted reconciliations. In fact, just before the accident, Esther had picked Denise up at her apartment and they were going to lunch to try to effect reconciliation. Unfortunately, Denise and Esther are now even further estranged as a result of the accident, and it appears that Denise intends to testify on behalf of the defendant.

Given the effect of Denise's expected testimony, we need to do our best to destroy her credibility. Please do the following:

Review the file and the research materials I have attached; in addition to the Federal Rules of Evidence, the *Christmas v. Sanders* case appears to be on point. Then prepare for me a cross-examination plan, focusing solely on impeaching her credibility. Attached is the office memorandum that specifies the format that must be used for drafting a witness cross-examination plan.

Freeman, Duke & Woolridge

3000 Paragon Place
Frederick, Columbia

MEMORANDUM   August 1, Yr-1

To: All Associates

From: Executive Committee

Re: Witness Cross-Examination Plan

When preparing a witness cross-examination plan, you should (1) state the topic of each series of questions; (2) under each topic, list the precise questions you propose be asked of the witness; (3) identify any objections you anticipate will be lodged by opposing counsel; (4) state the best response(s) to the objection; and (5) state the likely ruling. For example, the following was taken from the cross-examination plan in *Smith v. Jones*:

Topic: Witness' prior inconsistent statement concerning who had right of way.

Questions: Q. On direct, you testified that the light was green for Defendant, is that correct?

A. Yes.

Q. Immediately after the accident, you spoke to a police officer, is that correct?

A. Yes.

Q. You told the police officer that the light was green for Plaintiff, didn't you?

A. Yes.

Objections Anticipated: Hearsay.

Response: Prior inconsistent statement offered to show two stories, not for truth of either version.

Likely ruling: Admitted with limiting instruction.

ACCIDENT REPORT

Case No. 90-98762x

Vehicle 1 (Driver): Esther Dodson	Officer: Gorham
Vehicle 2 (Driver): None	Date: 1/15/Yr-1
Location: state rt. 17/1 mile E. Danforth	
Road/Weather Conditions: Road slippery/sleet falling	

Vehicle Description:

1. Yr-3 CEC Special
2. None

Witnesses:

Denise Johnston, sister of driver

Deer

Car

Guard Rail

NARRATIVE:

Officer arrived at scene following dispatch reporting single vehicle accident. Subject vehicle was located in ditch. Vehicle had crashed into guard rail but did not flip over. Driver, E. Dodson, remained in the front seat and was unconscious and appeared to have been struck in the neck by a large shard of glass. The only broken glass was the sunroof. Passenger, Denise Johnston, stated that she wasn't sure what happened. She said that her sister was driving under the speed limit. She thinks her sister lost control when she hit a deer that ran into the road. Ms. Johnston said that maybe the deer bounced off of the sunroof and shattered it, or that maybe her sister bounced off the seat and her head hit the sunroof. Ambulance arrived and removed driver and passenger to Danforth Community Hospital. No skid marks found. There was a large, dead deer next to the car. Spoke to Ms. Johnston after she was admitted to the hospital. Sister, Dodson, remains in coma. Ms. Johnston stated that her sister hit the sunroof because she wasn't wearing her seat belt.

United States District Court
Northern District of Columbia

Esther Dodson,
 	
                      Plaintiff,
v.
Canadian Equipment Company,
                    Defendant.
	C.A. No. 2182
	
	COMPLAINT FOR PERSONAL
	INJURIES

JURISDICTION

1. Plaintiff, Esther Dodson, is a citizen of the State of Columbia.

2. Defendant, Canadian Equipment Company, is incorporated under the laws of Canada with its principle place of business in Toronto, Ontario.

3. The matter in controversy exceeds, exclusive of interest and costs, the sum of fifty thousand dollars.

4. Jurisdiction is based on diversity of citizenship under 28 U.S.C. § 1332.

CLAIM I

5. Esther Dodson, age 38, was rendered paraplegic as the result of an accident on January 15, Yr-1.

6. At the time of the accident, Plaintiff was driving an automobile manufactured by Defendant.

7. The car Plaintiff was driving skidded on a snow-slick highway in Frederick, Columbia and struck and went through a guard rail. The impact with the guard rail caused the glass sunroof to shatter.

8. Despite the fact that she was wearing a seat belt, Plaintiff was injured when shattered glass from the sunroof in the car struck her, severing cervical nerves.

9. Defendant is the manufacturer of the car driven by Plaintiff.

10. Defendant was negligent in manufacturing the sunroof using tempered rather than laminated glass.

11. Plaintiff suffered general and special damages in excess of $2 million.

CLAIM II

12. Plaintiff realleges and incorporates by this reference the facts contained in paragraphs 1 through 11.

13. Defendant is strictly liable for Plaintiff's injuries.

WHEREFORE, Plaintiff prays judgment as follows:

1. That Plaintiff recover from Defendant general and special damages according to proof;

2. For costs of suit; and

3. For such other relief as the Court deems just and proper.

Elizabeth Duke
Elizabeth Duke
Attorney for Plaintiff
Date: June 1, Yr-1

United States District Court
Northern District of Columbia

Esther Dodson,

                                    Plaintiff, | C.A. No. 2182
              v. | ANSWER TO COMPLAINT
Canadian Equipment Company, | FOR PERSONAL INJURIES
                                    Defendant. |

ANSWER

1. In answer to Plaintiff's first claim, Defendant denies each and every allegation of paragraphs 8, 10 and 11.

2. In answer to paragraph 7, Defendant alleges that it lacks information and belief of the allegations thereof and, basing its denials thereon, denies each and every allegation thereof.

3. In answer to Plaintiff's second claim, Defendant hereby incorporates its answer to Plaintiff's first claim and, further, denies each and every allegation of paragraph 13.

AS AND FOR A FIRST AFFIRMATIVE DEFENSE to each of Plaintiff's claims, Defendant alleges that Plaintiff was not wearing her seat belt at the time of the accident.

WHEREFORE, Defendant prays judgment as follows:

1. That Plaintiff take nothing by the Complaint and that judgment be entered for Defendant;

2. For costs of suit; and

3. For such other relief as the Court deems just and proper.

Date: July 5, Yr-1   **Charles Smith**
                                      Attorney for Defendant

RIPKA INVESTIGATIONS

301 Main Street
Littleton, Columbia

MEMORANDUM   November 15, Yr-1

To: Elizabeth Duke

From: John Ripka, Investigator

Re: Denise Johnston Investigation Report

As you requested, I have conducted an investigation of Denise Johnston. As her sister has indicated, Ms. Johnston is a person with a checkered past.

Johnston has a criminal record of some significance. I have attached a copy. I do not have much information regarding the pending charge except that it seems to be the result of allegations of double billing in her business last year.

The Yr-4 conviction appears to be an incident of rowdy behavior at the beach.

The Yr-7 income tax fraud charge appears to have been dropped in exchange for Johnston paying income tax owed as well as a substantial penalty. The second time around, in Yr-3, Uncle Sam appears not to have been as forgiving. She pleaded guilty to a misdemeanor and was required to pay a $50,000 tax deficiency.

The Yr-9 conviction arose from possession of cocaine.

The Yr-11 conviction was the result of being part of a Medicare scheme in which the government was double billed.

Columbia Bureau of Investigation
Arrest Record

JOHNSTON,
DENISE

Social Security
No. 245-45-9834

DOB: 12/3/Yr-36

DATE	CHARGE	DISPOSITION
4/2/Yr-1	Fraud	Pending
7/28/Yr-3	Income tax fraud misde-meanor	Guilty plea
6/18/Yr-4	Drunk and disorderly misde-meanor	$50 fine
3/15/Yr-7	Income tax fraud	Charges dropped
6/27/Yr-9	Possession, controlled danger-ous substance, felony	Guilty plea, 6 months suspended
8/18/Yr-11	Medicare fraud	1 year probation

EXCERPT OF DEPOSITION OF DENISE JOHNSTON

Taken January 25, Yr-0

* * * *

BY ELIZABETH DUKE (Q): Would you tell us what occurred?

BY DENISE JOHNSTON (A): It's obvious, there was an accident.

Q: Would you tell us exactly what you saw occur?

A: My sister was speeding. She slammed into the guard rail and we were both pretty badly hurt. I was fortunate only because I was wearing the seat belt. She wasn't.

Q: Didn't you tell the police officer at the scene of the accident that you thought what caused the sunroof to shatter was that the deer bounced off the top of the car?

A: No, I told him only that my sister's head bounced off the sunroof because she wasn't wearing a seat belt.

* * * *

Q: You seem to be quite angry with your sister. Why?

A: Wouldn't you be? I couldn't work for six months. I'm trying to get my life back together. Then this comes along. For years she's been preaching about the way I live my life. She doesn't like the people I hang out with, blames me for some trouble I've had in the past. Then, pow. Just when I'm turning things around, starting to develop a reputation in the community for running a first rate home nursing service, she acts like an idiot and hurts us both.

Q: You intend to sue your sister for your damages, don't you?

A: Damn right I do.

Q: When did you form that intention?

A: In the ambulance when I realized that I was seriously injured.

* * * *

Q: A while ago, you mentioned your past. Let's turn to that. Our information is that 11 years ago you were convicted of aiding in double billing for Medicare. Is that right?

A: Look, that's over. I was put on probation. The doc went to jail for six months. The government's forgiven me, why can't my sister? What does this have to do with the accident anyway?

Q: What exactly was involved in that scheme?

A: Forget it. I run a straight home health service. The government pays me for my services. Why should you care?

Q: Well, let me ask about the drug conviction, then.

A: You can ask all you want. I'm not talking. This is just like my sister. Can't let up on anything. Good heavens, that was eight or nine years ago.

Q: Well, the pending fraud charge wasn't that long ago.

A: That's it. No more questions. I'm out of here.

EXCERPT FROM INTERROGATORIES TO CANADIAN EQUIPMENT COMPANY

* * *

INTERROGATORY NO. 5: Please identify any information acquired as the result of testing glass used for sunroofs subsequent to the time the product used in manufacturing the sunroof for the car in the present case was designed, formulated, tested, manufactured and sold by Canadian Equipment Company.

ANSWER: Defendant objects to this interrogatory on the ground that it is irrelevant to the subject matter of this litigation and will not lead to the discovery of any relevant and admissible evidence. Without waiving this objection, Defendant answers that tests were conducted to evaluate the comparative strength of tempered and laminated glass. Test results showed laminated glass to be stronger in resisting impact under crash conditions.

INTERROGATORY NO. 6: Identify all changes made in designing, planning, formulating, testing, preparing, manufacturing, packaging, warnings, labeling or instructing for the use of the sunroof in issue or any similar product, which changes were made subsequent to the time the sunroof in issue in this case was designed, formulated, tested, manufactured and sold by Canadian Equipment Company.

ANSWER: Defendant objects to this interrogatory on the ground that it is irrelevant to the subject matter of this litigation and will not lead to the discovery of any relevant and admissible evidence. Without waiving this objection, defendant answers that, as of six months ago, Canadian Equipment Company began using laminated glass in all automobile windows and sunroofs. A recall has been issued to replace sunroofs manufactured with tempered glass.

* * *

INTERROGATORY NO. 9: Please identify each expert witness defendant intends to call as a witness in this action and describe the proposed witness' education, training and experience upon which defendant asserts the witness is qualified as an expert.

ANSWER: Bradford Leyhe, J.D., PH.D. Dr. Leyhe's qualifications are stated in his curriculum vitae.

INTERROGATORY NO. 10: For each expert identified in the answer to the previous question, provide a summary of the expert's testimony.

ANSWER: Dr. Leyhe will testify to the following effect: CEC acted reasonably in using tempered glass rather than laminated glass to manufacture the sunroof. It would be possible to use laminated glass. However, it is not necessary to incur the added expense of doing so, because there would be no appreciable benefit. In the overwhelming number of cases, 100% protection from the type of injury that resulted in this case is ensured by use of a driver's seat belt such as was available in Ms. Dodson' car.

On the other hand, it is prudent to make windshields out of laminated glass because surface collisions from almost any side or angle can cause the windshield to shatter and a seat belt will not protect from the flying glass. Laminated glass is stronger than tempered glass, but that fact itself has a downside, i.e., if a vehicle occupant is hurled against a rigid pane that won't give, serious injury can still occur. That is just another way of saying that a seat best is a superior protective device.

There's another reason why use of laminated glass is probably not economically feasible for sunroofs: they are designed to be open in good weather. That's why people buy them. When the sunroof is open, the glass slides back into the metal roof, so there's no need to make it out of stronger material.

The main point in this case is that the injury suffered by the Plaintiff in this case could have been prevented if she'd been wearing a seat belt. An automobile manufacturer should not be required to make cars "idiot proof" or to design against freak, extremely remote occurrences.

LIBRARY

FEDERAL RULES OF EVIDENCE

Rule 401.   Definition of "Relevant Evidence."

"Relevant evidence" means evidence having any tendency to make the existence of any fact that is of consequence to the determination of the action more probable or less probable than it would be without the evidence.

Rule 402.   Relevant Evidence Generally Admissible; Irrelevant Evidence Inadmissible.

All relevant evidence is admissible, except as otherwise provided by the Constitution of the United States, by Act of Congress, by these rules, or by other rules prescribed by the Supreme Court pursuant to statutory authority. Evidence which is not relevant is not admissible.

Rule 403.   Exclusion of Relevant Evidence on Grounds of Prejudice, Confusion, or Waste of Time.

Although relevant, evidence may be excluded if its probative value is substantially outweighed by the danger of unfair prejudice, confusion of the issues, or misleading the jury, or by considerations of undue delay, waste of time, or needless presentation of cumulative evidence.

Rule 404.   Character Evidence Not Admissible to Prove Conduct; Exceptions; Other Crimes

(a)   **Character evidence generally.** — Evidence of a person's character or a trait of character is not admissible for the purpose of proving action in conformity therewith on a particular occasion, except:

(1)   **Character of accused.** — In a criminal case, evidence of a pertinent trait of character offered by an accused, or by the prosecution to rebut the same, or if evidence of a trait of character of the alleged victim of the crime is offered by an accused and admitted under Rule 404(a)(2), evidence of the same trait of character of the accused offered by the prosecution;

(2)   **Character of alleged victim.** — In a criminal case, and subject to the limitations imposed by Rule 412, evidence of a pertinent trait of character of the alleged victim of the crime offered by an accused, or by the prosecution to rebut the same, or evidence of a character trait of peacefulness of the alleged victim offered by the prosecution in a homicide case to rebut evidence that the alleged victim was the first aggressor;

(3)   **Character of witness.** — Evidence of the character of a witness, as provided in Rules 607, 608, and 609.

(b)   **Other crimes, wrongs, or acts.** — Evidence of other crimes, wrongs, or acts is not admissible to prove the character of a person in order to show action in conformity therewith. It may, however, be admissible for other purposes, such as proof of motive, opportunity, intent, preparation, plan, knowledge, identity, or absence of mistake or accident, provided that upon request by the accused, the prosecution in a criminal case shall provide reasonable notice in advance of trial, or during trial if the court excuses pretrial notice on good cause shown, of the general nature of any such evidence it intends to introduce at trial.

Rule 405.   Methods of Proving Character.

(a)   **Reputation or opinion.** — In all cases in which evidence of character or trait of character of a person is admissible, proof may be made by testimony as to reputation or by testimony in the form of an opinion. On cross-examination, inquiry is allowable into relevant specific instances of conduct.

(b)   **Specific instances of conduct.** — In cases in which character or a trait of character of a person is an essential element of a charge, claim, or defense, proof may also be made of specific instances of that person's conduct.

Rule 406.   Habit; Routine Practice.

Evidence of the habit of a person or of the routine practice of an organization, whether corroborated or not and regardless of the presence of eye witnesses, is relevant to prove that the conduct of the person or organization on a particular occasion was in conformity with the habit or routine practice.

Rule 608.   Evidence of Character and Conduct of Witness

(a)   **Opinion and reputation evidence of character.** — The credibility of a witness may be attacked or supported by evidence in the form of opinion or reputation, but subject to these limitations: (1) the evidence may refer only to character for truthfulness or untruthfulness, and (2) evidence of truthful character is admissible only after the character of the witness for truthfulness has been attacked by opinion or reputation evidence or otherwise.

(b)   **Specific instances of conduct.** — Specific instances of the conduct of a witness, for the purpose of attacking or supporting the witness' character for truthfulness, other than conviction of crime as provided in rule 609, may not be proved by extrinsic evidence. They may, however, in the discretion of the court, if probative of truthfulness or untruthfulness, be inquired into on cross-examination of the witness (1) concerning the witness' character for truthfulness or untruthfulness, or (2) concerning the character for truthfulness or untruthfulness of another witness as to which character the witness being cross-examined has testified.

The giving of testimony, whether by an accused or by any other witness, does not operate as a waiver of the accused's or the witness' privilege against self-incrimination when examined with respect to matters that relate only to character for truthfulness.

Rule 609.   Impeachment by Evidence of Conviction of Crime.

(a)   **General rule.** — For the purpose of attacking the character for truthfulness of a witness,

(1) evidence that a witness other than an accused has been convicted of a crime shall be admitted, subject to Rule 403, if the crime was punishable by death or imprisonment in excess of one year under the law under which the witness was convicted, and evidence that an accused has been convicted of such

a crime shall be admitted if the court determines that the probative value of admitting this evidence outweighs its prejudicial effect to the accused; and

(2) evidence that any witness has been convicted of a crime shall be admitted regardless of the punishment, if it readily can be determined that establishing the elements of the crime required proof or admission of an act of dishonesty or false statement by the witness.

(b)   **Time limit.** — Evidence of a conviction under this rule is not admissible if a period of more than ten years has elapsed since the date of the conviction or of the release of the witness from the confinement imposed for that conviction, whichever is the later date, unless the court determines, in the interests of justice, that the probative value of the conviction supported by specific facts and circumstances substantially outweighs its prejudicial effect. However, evidence of a conviction more than 10 years old as calculated herein, is not admissible unless the proponent gives to the adverse party sufficient advance written notice of intent to use such evidence to provide the adverse party with a fair opportunity to contest the use of such evidence.

Rule 613.   Prior Statements of Witnesses.

(a)   **Examining witness concerning prior statement.** — In examining a witness concerning a prior statement made by the witness, whether written or not, the statement need not be shown nor its contents disclosed to the witness at that time, but on request the same shall be shown or disclosed to opposing counsel.

(b)   **Extrinsic evidence of prior inconsistent statement of witness.** — Extrinsic evidence of a prior inconsistent statement by a witness is not admissible unless the witness is afforded an opportunity to explain or deny the same and the opposite party is afforded an opportunity to interrogate the witness thereon, or the interests of justice otherwise require. This provision does not apply to admissions of a party-opponent as defined in rule 801(d)(2).

Christmas v. Sanders
United States Court of Appeals for the Fifteenth Circuit (1992)

In this appeal from a civil judgment entered against her, defendant Lolita Sanders asks this court to grant her a new trial on the ground that the district judge erroneously excluded certain evidence of Plaintiff's prior conviction for rape. We affirm.

This case arises from a series of events that took place on the night of September 26, 1980. Defendant Sanders is a Chicago police officer. Sometime after 11:00 p.m., on September 26, Sanders changed from her police uniform into civilian clothes and left work at the 18th Street Precinct. That district is a high-crime area. Beyond this, the facts are sharply disputed, but the essence of the dispute is that an altercation occurred between plaintiff, Christmas, and defendant. Sometime during the altercation, Sanders drew her service revolver. Sanders claims she pointed it down to the ground hoping to calm the situation and that Christmas attempted to wrest the gun from her control. Christmas claims Sanders drew her revolver and shot him point blank.

The sole issue on appeal is whether the trial court erred in ruling that plaintiff's prior conviction for rape was inadmissible during the trial to impeach him. Under Rule 609, in a civil action, a prior felony conviction may only be admitted if the probative value is not outweighed by the prejudicial effect; it must be admitted under Rule 403, however, unless the prejudicial effect substantially outweighs probative value. Thus, Rule 609(a) leans heavily toward exclusion, while Rule 403 leans heavily toward admissibility.

To reverse, we must find the trial court's decision to be an abuse of discretion. This case turned solely on credibility, as the evidence consisted mainly of testimony by Christmas and Sanders, and each told markedly different versions. The jury verdict indicated that the jury credited most of Christmas' testimony and discredited the testimony of Sanders and several other witnesses, including one of Christmas' witnesses, who all said that they had seen Christmas and Sanders struggling in the intersection. Christmas produced no witnesses to substantiate his story that no struggle occurred between himself and Sanders. But the trial judge correctly noted that a conviction for rape was not highly probative of credibility. See *United States v. Larsen* (9th Cir.1979) (sex crimes "low on the list of crimes relating to veracity").

In addition, the district judge observed there was a possibility of substantial prejudice to the plaintiff because a jury might be unwilling to award damages to a convicted felon, presumably on the basis that Christmas was a "bad person." See *United States v. Haves* (2d Cir. 1977) (similarity of the subject of the prior conviction to the crime charged bears strongly on the possibility of prejudice, as inviting a direct inference of guilt rather than directing attention to credibility); *State v. Pinkham* (Me. 1978) (prior conviction for rape could not be admitted to impeach accused charged with another rape). Thus, there is ample basis in the record from which the district judge reasonably could have concluded that the prejudicial effect of the evidence substantially outweighed its probative value on the issue of credibility.

Also important to the issue of exclusion under Rule 403 would have been whether the prior felony conviction would have added much if anything in the way of impeachment. Christmas' own witness contradicted his testimony about no struggle and about where he fell down. Christmas admitted that he and his friend had been drinking that night and were wandering the streets later that evening in search of alcohol to consume. Christmas, a young man, admitted that he had been unemployed most of his adult working life and he did not ask any compensation for lost wages. Even without the rape conviction, Christmas presented the image of a man unlikely to lead a traditional upstanding life. Thus, the evidence of the rape conviction might also have been properly excluded under Rule 403 because, although probative, it was merely cumulative. See, e.g., *Furtado v. Bishop* (1st Cir. 1980) (exclusion under Rule 609(a)(1) was harmless error where judge admitted five other prior convictions of plaintiff and it was clear to the jury that plaintiff was a prison inmate; thus, defendant's attack on plaintiff's credibility could not have been impaired by the exclusion of this merely cumulative evidence). Based on the foregoing, we cannot say on the facts of this case that applying Rule 403 to Rule 609 in the manner the trial court did worked a manifest injustice on the defendant.

AFFIRMED.